More Food for Thought
Epigrams

More Food for Thought

Epigrams

By

Joseph Mileck

Pensive Oasis
Berkeley, California
2018

ISBN Print: 978-0-9982685-4-5
ISBN ebook: 978-0-9982685-5-2

Printed in the United States of America

Design and Layout: Rick Soldin (book-comp.com)

Pensive Oasis, Berkeley, California

Thought Begets Thought

Contents

Preamble

I was once very professional (1950-1991), taught German literature and language, and published scholarly books and articles. I am now quite ordinary, tend to my vegetable garden, and write poetry, epigrams and essays. Long preoccupied with the inner world of others, I finally began dwelling on my own. Retirement does unexpected things to both body and mind.

Since retirement, I have been wont to reflect upon what the French term *la condition humaine*, and upon the dour socio-political and cultural worlds in which we dwell. This preoccupation has made a buoyant skeptic of me, something of an optimistic pessimist, as evidenced by my past poetry and essays, and by my past and present epigrams.

All my reflections in literary garb are basically continuous attempts to clarify my thoughts about life. They are also meant to amuse and to prod their chance readers to reflect upon their own views of self and life.

Foreword

The Greek Epigram

O ur Western World's epigram—poetry at its briefest—has had a long and checkered history. It all began in Ancient Greece. At its earliest, the Greek epigram was but a commemorating inscription on a gravestone or monument. In time, simple inscription moved from stone to papyrus, became an elegiac couplet, and then ballooned to a four-to six-line poem. Somber one-line inscriptions became pithy verse: eulogistic, satirical and moralistic comment that often spared neither friend nor foe. Brevity, point and sting became and remained the intrinsic properties of Greece's long and rich trail of epigrams.

Meleager of Gadara was the foremost of ancient Greece's many author-compilers of epigrams. His compilation of the first century B.C.—a collection of epigrams of his and those of many of his predecessor epigrammatists—together with several subsequent compilations, became known in the 10th century as the *Greek Anthology*. This early collection of compilations, further augmented until the outset of the 17th century, was to have considerable influence on the 16th century vernacular literatures of Italy and France, and was even to attract a rush of scholarly interest as late as the 20th century: an English translation of the *Greek Anthology* appeared in 1916, followed by a French in 1928, and the anthology's cultural influence was widely scrutinized (e.g. James Hutten, *The Greek Anthology in Italy*, 1936; *The Greek Anthology of France*, 1946). This modern-day interest in Greece's ancient epigrams has continued to simmer to the very present.

The Latin Epigram

*U*nlike Greece, Ancient Rome was not blessed with a *Latin Anthology* and resultantly, most of the collections of epigrams written by many of its major writers—among them Domitius Marsus, Marcus Lucan, Cornifius and Cosconius—went the way that most things go. The foremost among Rome's authors whose epigrams survived were Gaius Valerius Catullus (84–54 B.C.), Decimus Junius (60–140 A.D.) and Marcus Valerius Martialis, Rome's master of the epigram. Martial was for Ancient Rome what Maleager of Gadora was for Ancient Greece.

The Latin epigram peaked in Martial's mordantly satirical asides. Though obviously much indebted to Greece's pioneering of the genre, his epigrams, and Latin epigrams in general, are unmistakingly Roman. In matter, they tend to be more personal, in manner, more terse, and in wit, more acridly satirical than their Greek counterparts. Martial spared neither the mighty nor the lowly, and neither friend nor foe. All were dispatched with abandon, some unabashedly eulogized and others caustically reduced, and liberal obscenities lent Martial's exposure of his society's faults and foibles a popular common touch.

In time, Martial's more than 1,500 extant epigrams became major models for both England's and France's epigrammatists. Indeed, the *Martial epigram* became the *European epigram*. Like Greece's, Rome's epigrams have continued to preoccupy translators and scholars to the present. Two volumes of English translations appeared in 1919 (W.C.A. Ker), three volumes of French translations followed in 1930 (H.J. Isaac), and the Latin epigram tradition has continued to attract scholarly attention (e.g., W.M Lindsay, 1929; C. Giarratano, 1951; R. Helm, 1951).

The European Epigram

*I*n the dark Middle Ages, European literary interest in the epigrammatic tradition of Greece and Rome was negligible. It was not until the Renaissance's reawakened interest in the literatures of Ancient Greece and Rome that Europe discovered and began to cultivate the epigram vernacularly. Martial's Latin pungent and often indecent epigrams served as major models for France's, England's and Germany's epigrammatists of the 17th and 18th centuries. Clément Marot (1496–1544) and Mellin de Saint Gelais (16th century) pioneered the French epigram, Ben Jonson (1573–1637) and Robert Herrick (1591–1674) ushered in the English epigram, and Friedrich von Logau set the German epigram on its way.

Europe's new literary interest spread rapidly. Many of France's, England's and Germany's poets began to explore the novel possibilities of the new genre. France's most prominent writers/intellectuals— among them, François Malherbe (1555–1625), François de La Rochefoucauld (1613–1680), Nicolas Boileau (1636–1700), Voltaire (1694–1718), Jean-Jacques Rousseau (1712–1778) and Victor Hugo (1812–1885)— took to the epigram like ducks to the water. Many of England's leading poets—among them, John Dryden (1631–1700), Matthew Prior (1664–1721), Jonathan Swift (1667–1745), Alexander Pope (1688– 1744), and Walter Savage (1775–1864)—and even a number of its prominent novelists—among them, George Meredith (1828–1909), Oscar Wilde (1854–1900), G.B. Shaw (1856–1950), and Hilaire Belloc (1870–1953)—became enthusiastic practitioners of the epigram. Germany's preoccupation, trailing that of France and England, peaked in the 18th century; (Gotthold Lessing, 1729–1781; Wolfgang Goethe, 1749–1832; and Friedrich Schiller, 1755–1805), gradually declined in the 19th century (Eduard Mörike, 1804–1875; and Friedrich Hebbel, 1813–1863), and has—like France and England's love affair with the epigram—but simmered on to the present.

France, England and Germany's present-day smoldering interest in the epigram may linger on and then eventually simply wither away, or it may again become the vigorous genre it once was, and hopefully sooner than later. What better setting for a likely renaissance of the epigram than the global social chaos of the 21st century. My own rush of some 7,600 epigrams (*A Medley of Piquant Poetry and Edgy Epigrams*, 2010; *More Salt and Pepper*, 2012; *Pensive Pauses*, 2016; and *More Food for Thought*, 2018) may become a part of this envisaged rebirth of the genre.

Definition

*P*rotean as it has been in its intent, matter, manner and tone, the epigram has to date defied fixed precise definition. Given that the epigram is but one of many generally familiar related terse expressions, definition by association, though perhaps less telling, is clearly more ready and inviting than definition by direct characterization.

There are the saying, saw, maxim, axiom, motto, adage, apothegm and aphorism, and all are terse familiar expressions of wit or wisdom or truth, all are humorous, satirical or paradoxical, and all are intent upon alerting, startling or shocking. It is to this family of popular utterances that the epigram belongs, and it is a discerning association with these common sayings that best defines the protean epigram.

A Family

Epigrams, proverbs, aphorisms and saws,
Maxims, adages, sayings and mottoes,
All say much in their brevity,
All words of wit and words of wisdom,
All weighty in their philosophical gaze,
All are informative and all tease thought,
All easily memorized, all readily recalled,
And all should be heeded though all can be challenged.

More Food for Thought

*T*he 3,100 or more epigrams of the present collection and the some 4,500 previously published (*A Medley of Piquant Poetry and Edgy Epigrams*, 2010; *More Salt and Pepper. Poems and Epigrams*, 2012; *Pensive Pauses. Epigrams and Poems*, 2016)) were inspirationally indebted to the European epigram, but only loosely mindful of the intent, matter, manner and tone of their models. In their intent to alert and to invite or compel reciprocal thought, these epigrams, unlike the traditional epigram, are general and mild rather than personal and sharp; in their preoccupation with the human and social condition, their moralizing, psychologizing and philosophizing, and in their focus on religion and human values, they are again more general than personal. With their characteristic end- and internal rhymes, their common alliterations and parallel structures, these predominantly one-line epigrams tend to be more terse and more poetic than the traditional European epigram. In tone they are also less crusty and less blunt.

May the epigrams and poems of *More Food for Thought* chance on curious minds, and may they stir to advantage!

August 2018

EPIGRAMS

Read slowly and with care,
Concur or issue take,
Then your own thoughts pen,
For thinkers we are all.

Pensive Pauses

*E*very youngster and most every oldster is something of a performer.

Obsessions are possessions.

Wisdom that is taught, quickly comes to nought.

The world is what it is because humans are what they are.

Chance is yours to accept and choice is yours to make.

Know that to learn is to grow.

Save it, don't blow it.

Commonality makes for community, difference rouses hostility.

Commonality makes for compatibility.

Omniscience and omnipotence are aspirations, not realities.

Feed need, starve your want.

Request and smile, don't demand and rile.

Don't ask a fish to fly.

Don't eat what you can't swallow.

The healthy are the truly wealthy.

To ask the right question is as important as to give the right answer.

Deception diminishes both deceived and deceiver.

Convenience prevails, necessity pales.

Submission is an admission of contrition.

The physically strong are too often the morally weak.

Truth is but what is deemed to be truth.

Imagined beliefs become absolute truths.

Acquisitiveness dehumanizes, inquisitiveness debases.

Better to prevent than to cure.

Illness sensitizes, health stabilizes.

Fitness keeps sickness at bay.

Fitness checkmates illness.

Hesitate and cogitate before you bloviate.

Too many nobodies would be somebodies.

There is no up but for a down.

The thin are in and the stout are out.

It is not who you are but what you are.

Too many definitions opine more than they define.

The past is a presence no longer present.

Peace and war are foretaste of heaven and hell.

The genders are both attracted to each other and suspicious of each other.

Greed has little to do with need.

Love endears, will compels.

Too many are too busy doing nothing to do something.

Simplify, don't amplify.

Memories are paintings, not photographs.

Read between the lies.

But for things there would be no space, and but for change there would be no time.

Christianity is spent, Islam is rent, and the whole world is in foment.

Better to be empty than to be full of oneself.

The Black Community *has a problem*, and the White Community *is the problem*.

Lies are compulsive, truths are impulsive.

Lies are a fact, and truths are fancy.

Bodies are abused, and minds are too little used.

Commonality becalms, difference bestirs.

Self-justification is common, self-knowledge is rare.

Some never start learning, and some never stop learning.

Better to step aside than to collide.

A good diet is the best of medicines.

We are all common clay, and differ only in our social glazing.

We who turn the other cheek are seen as weak.

Stir the pot, brew a thought.

A clash of cultures is a clash of religions.

Celebrate the possible, don't just mourn the impossible.

It's nice to be important, and it's important to be nice.

As much freedom as possible, and as much regulation as necessary!

There are the thinkers and the feelers, and then there are the feeling thinkers and the thinking feelers.

Don't equivocate, elucidate.

Insinuation is a devious device.

Infatuation is a blossom that never was a bud.

Life is what we make of it, not what it makes of us.

To care is to worry.

Democracy should be spread by the force of law, and not by the law of force.

To emote less and to reflect more, will preclude much verbal war.

Too much ends before it begins.

Effort deserves recognition, success merits praise.

There are more divides than there are bridges.

Change—physical or mental—is as good as rest.

Bridges include and walls exclude.

Each has many masks.

Sober times demand sober minds.

You have to stir the pot to brew up a thought.

Stir your little pot, or remain a nought.

No one would be a nobody.

What is not known or understood, is commonly feared and hated.

Know your better self, then be that better self.

But a few live, the many exist.

Clowns entertain, fools are a pain.

Diversity spells controversy.

To train is to prepare for a job, to educate is to prepare for life.

Incarcerate fewer and rehabilitate more

But for their curt striking expression, most esteemed truths would fall by the wayside.

One person's gain is another person's pain.

Don't depend on the many, and don't trust the superior few.

Savor, don't devour, smile, don't growl.

One person's necessities are another person's luxuries.

Desperate hope trumps livid hate.

For some, work is play, and for others, play is work.

Every choice has its price.

Noise distracts and agitates, music attracts and elevates.

Certainty is absurdity, and doubt is rationality.

Conventional truths are convenient lies.

Where there is a will, there's a way, but it is not always paved.

Change is life's sole constant.

To know, is to know that one cannot know.

Love is life's most familiar of fantasies.

Better to assist than to resist.

It's always the different, that makes the difference.

Much is rearranged, little is ever changed.

Don't beat what is already dead.

Of our many literary genres, common gossip is probably the most common.

The tall have their advantage, and the short have theirs.

Silent expectations are all abominations.

Better to lie low than to fly high.

Truths are fluid, not fixed.

Better to refrain than to complain.

To be yourself you must first know yourself.

Too much *I* leaves too little room for *we*.

Creations refresh their creators.

Technology fares well, psychology knows better.

Technology is simple-minded, psychology is open-minded.

Be inspired by truth, and aided by fact.

Think a good thought, and do a good deed.

To lighten your burdens, shed your airs.

To be bold is to be brash, to be brave is to be rash.

Daily ablution was olden times' daily solution.

Many an electronic device has become but absorbing vice.

Anticipation is sweet elation.

Electronic devices are a rage, except for the old and sage.

To lie or cheat, is never meet.

Epigrams are keys that tantalize and tease.

To envy another, is to belittle the self.

Most would be what they are not.

Stone memorializes, earth eternalizes.

What is consciousness but miraculous awareness.

All creatures have their telltale features.

Well-being and old age, rarely dwell on the same page.

The few lead and the many are led.

While the fat sit grim, the slim are in the swim.

There are the loud-mouthed mindless, and then there are the
soft-spoken thoughtful.
And ne'er the twain will meet.

Most thoughts are prematurely aborted, but few are full-term births.

Emotions are ultimately life's major determinants.

Those who chatter all day, have nothing to say.

The fat are abhorred, and the thin are deplored.

Gods are of mankind's imagination, and not of its ratiocination.

To do is to be.

Justice is hope, prayer, and pain.

To heed need and to curb want, is to be left less distraught and more content.

For the few, life is pomp and ceremony, for the many, life is toil and agony.

What lives, kills, and what kills, lives.

We preach peace and order, and espouse war and chaos.

To be selfish is as natural as to be hungry.

For the temperamental, life can be a rollercoaster, for the placid, life can be a peaceful pond.

The cultures and civilizations of our world would never have seen the light of day, but for our world's religions.

One need not be lonely, when alone.

Masochists are at odds with themselves, and sadists with others.

Everything is ever changing, yet nothing is ever different.

A now and here, presupposes a then and there.

Pastime for some is lost time for others.

Overtime is better for one's wealth than for one's health.

Good and bad are judgment more than fact.

The envious rarely ever smile, the content rarely never smile.

The daring don't think, and the thinkers don't dare.

Life is a presence, and death is an absence.

Misfortune is countered, when good fortune is encountered.

We do what we do, because we can't do otherwise.

In decease, all ceases.

Better to do what one wills to do, than to do what others will one to do.

Bold and outrageous words precede hesitant and mild actions.

To know little, is to feel small, and to know much, is to feel big.

To focus on the mass is to lose sight of the individual.

Pre-emptive attack only invites counterattack.

Reaction calls for reflection.

To be vindictive, is quite instinctive.

To assume the worst, is to prepare for the worst.

The thoughts of another are the thoughts of a brother.

A big heart and an open mind are of a kind.

To deplore is rational, to abhor is emotional.

If it's taboo, it's not for you.

In doubt, be open-minded and big-hearted.

To take to heart, is a good start.

One can't go forward by going backward.

Love prizes and hate despises.

To flirt is to tease more than to please.

Sex is of the body, love is of the mind.

Take care of your health, and your health will take care of you.

The lazy of mind outnumber the lazy of body.

When Heaven laments, Hell foments.

God embraces, the Devil effaces.

Sex can both hex and vex.

Sex is flesh and lust, love is spirit and compassion.

Sex takes and rakes, love gives and forgives.

Nothing will be that never was.

Life is rough, but humans are tough.

Toe the line or pay a fine.

To be informed, is to be forewarned.

Do good for good, and not for thanks.

To be fit in mind, is as important as to be fit in body.

Truth hath two faces and no basis.

Optimism energizes, pessimism lethargizes.

Hate has never been out of date.

All in life is provisional, like it or not.

When the boss is away, the workers play.

Hearers are many, heeders are few.

Needs are numbered, wants are numberless.

All is more chance than choice.

Little is what it seems to be.

The mind rages, when the body ages.

To think of what others think and to think back, is to be on the right track.

Reason alone is too confining, and passion alone is too blinding.

One can be spiritually rich, though materially poor.

Wealth can be as much pain as gain.

Heed the line or pay a fine.

Don't take slight, when there's no slight.

The more you shout, the less you say.

Chance is obfuscation, cause and effect are explanation.

Heaven and hell are here, not there.

The healthy are the wealthy, the sick are the poor.

The felt is no less real than the thought.

Noise stuns, silence numbs.

Birth, life and death are chance not choice.

Romance and dance invigorate, work and worry enervate.

Children should play and work, adults should work and play.

It is sane to neglect neither body nor brain.

To set the table, is to whet the appetite.

An addiction is an affliction that knows no satisfaction.

Freedom is merited, not inherited.

Not to think, is not to have thoughts.

Texture and taste are not a waste.

Haste is all too often but waste.

Too much thought ends in nought.

The distraught rarely achieve aught.

To know much, generally, is to know little, specifically.

Humans are still more animal than human.

Much is known, but little is understood.

Men prefer to mount, women to be mounted.

The make is as flawed as its maker.

The wise think, fools know.

Perception is ever in need of correction.

A dance will life enhance.

One does best, when not stressed.

To unlearn, is to learn.

Attraction appetizes, interaction satisfies.

When love sours, hatred flowers.

People who mean well, are rarely treated well.

The not done can be as reprehensible as the done.

All is in flux, but flux itself.

Let live what wills to live, and let die what cannot live.

Think your private thoughts, and weigh those of others.

To perplex, one need but to complex.

To remain alive is a universal drive.

Aloneness is lot, loneliness is plight.

Sex is to service and to be serviced.

The brainy are rarely brawny, and the brawny are rarely brainy.

A bad conscience is a good nuisance.

Too few really live, and too many just exist.

Minor decisions often have major consequences.

We do what we do, because we are what we are.

Competition makes some and breaks others.

To know oneself one must live oneself, and to live oneself, one must know oneself.

Life's sweet intensities take their bitter toll.

Too much choice is as burdensome as too little choice is irksome.

Smiles are invitation, frowns are rejection.

To ossify is to die.

To take umbrage is to invite carnage.

Wealth enjoys justice, poverty suffers injustice.

Punishment is retaliation, not rehabilitation.

One suffers one's lot, like it or not.

For all too many, God's a chill and the Devil's a thrill.

To mythicize is to eternalize.

Reason constrains and imagination entertains.

Ablution washes away, and absolution spirits away.

Digital addiction has become a social affliction.

Most possibilities do not become realities.

Nationalism preaches, and patriotism teaches.

Better to teach than to preach.

Play energizes, and work enervates

Civility is not servility.

Hope energizes, and despair lethargizes.

The unknown is mysterious, the known tedious.

The more informed, the greater one's range of thought.

We are but means to an end and, that end is life.

Rich or poor, we come and go from birth to death.

Too few see, though eyes they have.

To talk too much, is to say too little.

Old age dims the mind, and deforms the body.

An open mind is hard to find.

Wealth may be a burden, poverty is a blight.

When health fails, all else pales.

The hurried are our worried.

Clouds are real, the sky is a lie.

Not to know agony, is not to know bliss.

Do your best, better you cannot do.

Attraction and distraction walk hand in hand.

Better to try and fail, than to quake and wail.

To do good is to do well.

Laughter relaxes, and anger taxes.

A good deed is a sown seed.

Heed your need, and daunt your want.

To know better, is to fare better.

Animals of a kind, link and bind.

Writers are wonderful liars.

A non-belief is also but another belief.

Chance is a dance, that oft ends in romance.

Conveniences beget inconveniences.

Good deeds are good seeds.

Weep and frown, then laugh and smile.

Generosity and gratitude bind and bless.

Person is primary, station is secondary.

We are what we choose to be.

Age alone does not make sage.

Knowledge is appreciated, wisdom is prized.

To wage war, is to appreciate peace.

The old are not bold, and the young are not wise.

Atone we can, undo we can't.

What is sin for some, is fun for others.

Attractions are no less distractions.

Empathy binds and apathy blinds.

The physically and mentally alive, are the most likely to thrive.

Challenge is cerebral, opposition is vocal.

Science tests, religion asserts.

Incremental change is acceptable, radical change upsets.

Change excites, and stability comforts.

War energizes, peace lethargizes.

Changelessness knows neither time nor space.

To underestimate the self, is to overestimate the other.

Introverts have their inner retreat, extroverts have their outer playground.

Self-esteem is as much determined by family as it is by society.

Life is a meld of chance and choice.

All is well, when gains balance losses.

The Electronics Age's world of virtuality, has for too many become life's reality.

The all too many who but exist, are our living dead.

Physical pleasure is more ready than mental pleasure.

Substance attracts interaction, appearance invites attraction.

Life is a meld of grief and joy.

Expectation spawns exasperation.

A gift in need is a joy indeed.

Wisdom is a rare by-product of a fully-lived life.

Humans ponder and wonder, things seduce and sedate.

Men are inclined to roam and women prefer a home.

The killing of human beings, legally or otherwise, and for whatever reason and by whatever means, is mankind's wrong of wrongs.

Brain is esteemed, brawn is embraced.

Heaven knows no wants or needs.

Kindness is uplifting, anger is upsetting.

The bold strut, the timid stare.

Life's givens are life's determinants.

To spend is a chore, and to save is a bore.

Clean windows serve both those who peek out, and those who peer in.

Pathways are inviting while freeways are daunting.

Be a *be* and not a *seem-to-be*.

Sport should be pleasant recreation, not fierce competition.

Education is thought-minded, commercialism is
purse-persuaded.

Satisfaction depends upon expectation.

The right hand takes, and the left hand gives.

All is as meant to be.

Chance and choice are compelling force.

What is, is change in changelessness.

It's not right, nor is it wrong,
For what is right, is also wrong.

The present recalls the past, and anticipates the future.

Much talent is born of psychological compensation.

Achievers are beavers.

Dire prediction is a common affliction.

First thoughts are persuading, second thoughts are convincing.

Simplicity is felicity.

To explain is but to make plain.

Brain and brawn are co-dependent equals.

When cultures wane, truths pale.

Truths are transients, not residents.

When belief flags, culture sags.

To doubt is as natural as it is to believe.

Morality is for the poor plurality.

Good deeds are like good seeds.

A stitch in line is right fine.

Advice can be two-faced.

The crowd should have its day, but not its way.

Sympathy is good, compassion is better.

Truths are belief, and facts are circumstance.

Earth is a trying reality, and heaven is a glorious fiction.

Female charm and wiles ably counter male brawn and aggressiveness.

Say your say, then stay or go away.

Opinions are ballast, ideas are compass.

It is not enough just to be alive.

Books are wondrous windows.

Life is fine, when body and mind combine.

Bodies that tire more rapidly, heal more slowly.

One is only as old as one thinks and feels.

Kindness rewards both parties.

Birds of a kind each other find.

To give of one's little, is to give much of oneself.

Crowd thinking is self-promoting, not thought-provoking.

Too many talk too much, and say too little.

The few have too much, and the many have too little.

To comfort in sorrow and to aid in need, is to be a friend in deed.

The old are as given to the past as the young are taken with the future.

Brawn groans and brain sighs.

When work becomes play, every day becomes a holiday.

Work and play should share the day.

Character will show, when ill winds blow.

Be somebody and not a nonentity.

Too much said is designation and not explanation.

To inform is addition, to explain is calculus.

Do your best and then rest.

To have opinions is good, to have informed opinions is better.

Change and time are cause and effect.

Things and space are cause and effect.

Digitalia's espoused novelty and convenience, demands much and affords little.

One hand washes the other.

Hardly thought before wrought.

Expectations invite vexations.

Life's prime drive is to stay alive.

The silent treatment speaks loudly.

Mankind created its Creator.

Do it or you will rue it.

Some listen and see, more just hear and look.

Juvenile technology and single-minded business world, have fashioned a society destined to self-destruct.

People are rarely what they deem themselves to be.

People commonly think more emotionally than rationally.

Dwell on message, not on messenger.

Some are thinkers, others are doers, and too many just are.

To take serious issue with the socio-political scene of one's country, is not to dirty one's own nest or to hate it.

Better to do something poorly than to do nothing.

Government of the people, by the people and for the people, is an ideal never realized.

To function ably and effectively, Democracy has to be buttressed by Autocracy.

Democracy is a touch of Heaven that chanced to fall on earth.

Autocracies are a natural form of government, and democracies, in marked contrast, are an ideal form of government.

The riven and driven are sooner or later left rent and spent.

The wise are at peace with self and world.

To be someone, one must first become someone.

Discussion may attenuate, quarrel will acerbate.

We are born but once and we die but once, and contentions to the contrary are but wishful thinking.

That men are becoming more like women, and women more like men, is a good cultural omen.

The married are more harried than the single.

Our Judeo-Christian God will survive the collapse of the Western World, but only to reappear in a new guise and touting a new gospel.

Aloneness is existential lot, loneliness is psychology.

Relent and repent, when morally spent.

Vent your anger, and then get on with life.

Not to remember is a loss to mourn.

Ability and confidence spell competence.

Facts are but information.

Some are virtually dead before they have actually died.

To bend is not to break.

Mankind has managed to survive and even thrive, despite life's many perils and because of resilience and tenacity.

Humans are primarily of the body and little of the spirit.

Biblically, things of the body are dirty, things of the spirit are immaculate.

Too many are dead before they have died.

Fancies intoxicate, facts sober.

Self-defensive self-examination is largely self-deception.

Indolence has its recompense.

Our why's are our woes.

Neither alcohol nor tobacco are a problem in Heaven.

Hell must be one enormous barbecue.

To pursue perfection is to invite dejection.

Criticism can be bile or concern.

Not to ask is not to know.

It is wise to ponder life's why's.

Hate is what it is, and love is one of many things.

One is the poorer for one's greed.

Envy the decent, not the wealthy.

Better but to inch forward, than to remain fixed.

Ready answers are more comfort than assurance.

Anything that promises too much, affords too little.

Planets are of cosmic eruption, civilizations are human creations.

What the eyes see is actuality, what the mind stores is virtuality.

The discriminately good are acceptable, the indiscriminately good are laudable.

To do what one wills is to accept what one gets.

To do good is to be good.

It takes two to tangle.

Poverty plagues the poor, and wealth afflicts the rich.

When there is need, respond in deed.

Attention and comprehension walk hand in hand.

Money has become paramount, all else is secondary.

Money is a big curse and a small blessing.

Self-serving pretence is a common social offence.

Each is a constant becoming from birth to death.

Birth is a surprise, death is an inevitability.

Anger suppressed, is anger not addressed.

Insanity and genius have common roots.

Contentment is to have, and discontent is not to have.

Handymen are less skilled than they are handy.

Revenge only seeds more revenge.

Pain is a blessing no less than a curse.

The normal sates, the abnormal baits.

Naysayers should be gainsaid.

The crippled find the crippled.

Naysayers and gainsayers are birds of a feather.

Too many talk too much and say too little.

We are what we want and need, and what we take and give.

Goodness, though a rare commodity, has on Wall Street found no popularity.

Racism will not take cover until there is no other.

Things don't change, they morph.

Output is contingent upon input.

Unqualified freedom is freedom's undoing.

Freedom untethered is freedom's demise.

Life's humanization has yielded to life's digitalization.

Digitalization is civilization, not culture.

Digitalia's reification of civilization, is an abomination.

Everybody shouts and nobody hears.

The best rarely rest.

To know everything about everything, is to know nothing about anything.

Information fuels, thought transfigures.

Readily and generally accessible masses of information about anyone and anything, is a nightmare not a dream.

Too little starves, too much cloys.

Each happens, and to each, things happen.

Most of what most say or do, is of little ado.

The hoi-polloi are those who never were, and the hoity-toity are those who would be.

Flaunted wares attract words and stares.

Know where it is, and put it back to where it was.

The certainty of ignorance is appalling.

Bigger jails don't reduce crime.

The proud are all too loud, and the weak are too meek.

Change is inevitable and time is incessant.

We are what we are, what we were, and what we will be.

Mystically, we are oneness in multiplicity and timelessness in time.

Propagation is the passion that has sustained all living things.

Mankind has dreamed up the most fantastic of explanations to account for the unaccountable.

Truths are fashioned to satisfy curiosity and need.

We do not live by bread alone, fiction has always sustained us.

The fleet of foot survive in the wild, and the quick of mind cope well in civilization.

True love takes gently, and gives freely.

The bold will take and hold, the meek will yearn and seek.

There is no time but there is change.

Appetites curbed, are appetites controlled.
Appetites sated, are appetites in control.

Dogs growl, cats hiss, humans grumble, and life goes on.

We learn and unlearn, and not always for the better.

Democracy is theoretically extolled and practically abused.

Most become what they become and do what they do, to compensate for deficiencies and to counter their inadequacies.

Body language is often more telling than verbal language.

To be socially fair is aim not goal.

Law is state morality and morality is church law.

Courts don't dispense justice, they but make decisions.

Cautious response is *why*, curiosity's retort is *why not*.

Good is good, when good is commonly good.

Expect no less of yourself than of others.

It is mankind itself and not god or the devil, that stirs the pot of life.

Individuals are by and large of their own doing and undoing.

Lip service is disservice.

To perform, is a need to attract.

Health, like wealth, is most appreciated when lost.

Gender is a private matter and not a public issue.

The strong and the cunning survive, the weak and witless succumb.

The poor skimp and sigh, the rich wallow in their wealth.

Civility has become a casualty.

The new-normal has brass knuckles.

Humans are more devil- than God-like.

Bigger is of itself not better.

Life is strife and knife.

Time heals all wounds.

Wars settle nothing and destroy everything.

Not to be forgotten by the living, is little consolation for the dead.

Reparations do not atone for, or undo the untoward said and done.

When business waxes, morality wanes.

Farsightedness is a rare human attribute.

Nothing was created, all just became.

Alternative truths are convenient lies.

The more we learn, the less we know.

To educate is cultural, to train is industrial.

Be yourself and not what others would have you be.

Captain your own ship.

Circumstances should be controlled and not be controlling.

Don't allow the things that distress you to possess you.

To be resilient is to be able to cope.

Acceptance precludes belligerence.

Too much is often too little.

Be yourself and not your would be.

If you purge the urge, there'd be no splurge.

But for change, there'd be no time.

An urge is an itch, that needs a scratch.

When morality loses its grip, criminality takes over the ship.

Assertions invariably attract their denials.

To socialize is to conventionalize.

To rely too much upon others, is to expect too little of the self.

Life has its traffic lights, heed them.

Trust until there is reason to distrust.

Epigrams, like proverbs, are both amusing and compelling.

The done cannot be undone.

To wage war, is to slaughter and to be slaughtered.

Reflection is more distraction than attraction.

Children are a sweet burden.

To be reflexive is natural, to be reflective is cultural.

Wise it is, to heed needs and to curb wants.

Absolute patriotism is absolute madness.

Trainers train, teachers educate.

If you think before you act, it's unlikely that you will have to retract.

To go one's way and to do one's thing, is often less quest than plain fling.

Idle hands and lazy minds are common kinds.

Challenge stimulates and success elates.

Too much sleep will leave mind dull and body weak.

Fists are for fight and legs are for flight.

The heart beats steadily, the mind flits erratically.

Be brash, if you will, but not rash.

Freedom is as much responsibility as it is privilege.

Good will is silver, compassion is gold.

To have is to be, to have not is to be not.

To go one's way and to do one's thing can be challenge or just fling.

Discretion is the better part of reciprocity.

When life gets tough, humans get rough.

It is not meet to cheat.

Fastidiousness is personally irking, lasciviousness is socially appalling.

The messy see too little, and the finicky see too much.

Royalty has become a virtual antiquity.

The female of most species has always been, and still is, something of an underdog.

Not to know is to be blind.

Not to feel is to be dead.

To know is to be in the flow.

Let live what wills to live,
Let die what cannot live.

Be informed, be reflective, and be a decent human being.

One can do it, if one sets one's mind to it.

To know too little of the past, is to be too little prepared for the present.

A dejected, "If it's not this, it's that," changes nothing for the better.

The mind needs its belief no less than the body its bread.

Time will tell, but few will heed.

Problems wished away, don't go away.

Stand tall and don't fall.

The sleazy are rarely queasy.

Small talk and small minds go hand in hand.

An impaired body is no less a loss than an impaired mind.

Tenacity befits the young, and sagacity befits the old.

Traditionally, the male indulged and the female abstained.

Teachers are but older and more informed students.

If brevity is the soul of wit, then expansiveness is the stuff of boredom.

Life has its many losers and its few winners.

Strife began when life began.

What is, is a meld of the past, present and the future.

Too many leading politicians are but comic-strip reality.

Neither what happened nor what did not happen, can ever be erased.

Love, like truth, is an ill-defined concept.

Trust only when trust is trustworthy.

Better to begin anew, than to continue to fume and spew.

Be what you are and not what you pretend to be.

When hell breaks loose, make for heaven.

To disarm, one need but charm.

Even the nobodies are somebody to someone.

In due time, even the most celebrated of somebodies become nobodies.

Cling we do, but go we will.

Sex is more than just three thrusts and a sigh.

Most persons are neither as good as they believe, nor as bad as others would have them be.

Praise attracts praise, and criticism attracts criticism.

The majority can be as wrong as it can be right.

Politicians bloviate too much, and legislate too little.

Men will and women would.

Better to inspire than to intimidate.

The love of sports and the business of sports, are worlds apart.

Profit is the name of the business game.

Some want to hear, more want to be heard.

Too many talk too much and say too little.

Action and activity should not be equated.

The loud are heard but little heeded.

Pretence can be subtle defence or only offence.

Together, mental and physical activity make for good health and longevity.

Wanting sleep leaves wanting health in its wake.

Patriotism and militarism are a deadly meld.

Wars are not won or lost but both won and lost.

We know ever more and grasp ever less.

Reach does not always exceed grasp

To hurry is to harry.

Know that you know less than you know.

Timidity is psychology, not morality.

Virtuality is rapidly becoming our reality.

Some think, some do, and many do neither.

Thinking doers and doing thinkers are society's rudder and ballast.

The blame game is a lame game.

Writers think and write, readers read and think.

To know another is to know the self that much better.

The easy route first rewards, then takes its toll.

Success and failure are but judgment, and judgment is but fallible opinion.

Learn from experience or re-experience your experience.

Diligence is application, indolence is indulgence.

One man's gain should not be another man's loss.

But for the night, there would be no day.

Acts beget acts and thoughts beget thoughts.

Age cripples the body and blurs the mind.

Don't forget, but never rue,
Let be what was and greet the new.

Yourself to fulfill,
Grow you must
And grow you will!

Youth aspires and age inspires.

Law does not eliminate the unlawful, it only curtails it.

Give what you can and take what you must.

Help both the needy good and the needy bad.

To envy or to demean others is to disparage the self.

Love what you should not hate, and hate what you should not love.

Death leaves behind but a treasured fading shadow in the mind.

To nurture treasured memories, is to re-live life.

Diplomatic ventures usually attenuate, strong arm tactics always
infuriate.

Dignity is a rarity, earned not bought.

Wars make, don't solve problems.

Epigrams stimulate, tweets titillate.

Wars destroy randomly and kill wantonly.

Reality, though ever changing, is never different.

Impartiality elicits cheers, partiality elicits jeers.

Sanctions don't quench, they stoke.

Promises harmonize, threats antagonize.

The pen is love and life, the sword is hate and death.

Perfection is an ideal, not something real.

Right it is to be contrite, better never to have gone astray.

Curiosity should remain mindful of virtuosity.

Generosity has for too many become but a curiosity.

Dignity is not a commodity.

Best for the wayward is correction, not punishment.

Prisons should rehabilitate more and punish less.

We curb and are curbed.

You are your failures no less than your successes.

Be what you are and not what others would have you be.

Curb your biases or be curbed by your biases.

Each is two: The private and the public self.

When religion loses its grip, society becomes a ship without rudder and ballast.

Religion is the most awe-inspiring of mankind's many noble fictions.

The ideal motivates, and the real operates.

Give liberally where there is need, and sparingly where there is want.

Every religion can learn from every other religion.

Experience is life's best teacher.

The dark skies are never without their bright stars.

One person's attraction is another person's distraction.

Christianity's God is a very human God fashioned by humans.

Levity should go hand in hand with brevity.

To play with fire is to be burned by fire.

Nothing is for nothing, contrary to the contrary.

Humans are clearly not apes, but also just as clearly of a kind.

It's not the product itself, but its marketing, that carries the day.

Given each person's uniqueness, everyone is essentially a stranger to every other.

Scrutinize hearsay and utilize informed opinion.

Scrutinize and analyze, don't just fantasize.

Romance is flirtatious, marriage is dedication.

When womb is removed, buggy is taken out and playpen is left in.

Be a hugger, not a bugger.

Know thyself is more easily said than done.

Not to know is to be disoriented and to be bewildered.

Mankind knows much, but it has never known enough.

Mankind's capacities have always fallen short of the ultimately possible.

To say *can't* is not to try.

To have tried is to have learned.

Failure is a bitter pill that leaves one the better for it.

Failure is the first step on the road to success.

What's not tight, does not squeak.

Not to socialize, is to fossilize.

We eat because we have to, and think because we choose to.

Material wellbeing and cultural wellbeing should go hand in hand.

If it barks, it isn't a cat.

Some people eat just to eat.

Too many simply do what they want to do, rather than what they are morally obliged to, or legally compelled to do.

Much is too much, when little is enough.

Life is flow and death is ebb.

Brows tend to frown when the chips are down.

Actions not consonant with words, are good cause for a reflective pause.

Study changes lives, and changed lives change society.

Not controversy but debate should be on the public's plate.

Better a banal nobody than a questionable somebody.

The more different the partners, the more challenging the marriage.

To unlearn is almost as trying as to learn.

Spend when necessary and save when possible.

To become informed is to begin to think on a broader and higher plane.

To promise something to everyone is not to give anything to anyone.

Ambiguity is more ploy than toy.

To be trusted, you yourself must trust.

Lucubrations instruct, adumbrations baffle.

When in order, calmly pocket pride, and quickly extend apology.

When things go askew, it's time to begin anew.

When you go bust, call for help you must.

To break it, is to own it.

Life is a problem, and death is its solution.

Cherish both the fruits of brawn and the fruits of brain.

Share with a less fortunate other, when your cup runneth over.

The milk of human kindness needs no pasteurizing.

Criminals have their prisons, and the poor have their ghettos.

Conformity is comfort, diversity is excitement.

As robots gain, humans wane.

Absolute freedom peaks in absolute anarchy.

Morality's left empty-handed, immorality is loot-burdened.

Forbearance is feminine, outrage is masculine.

Anarchy is born of absolute freedom.

Masculine violence is commonly but a therapeutic release of pent-up energy.

Men advance and women recoil.

Technology's ever more sophisticated electronic devices threaten to become ever more impressive and ever less practical.

Most only know of, or about another, few really know another.

The hypersensitive live on pins and needles of their own making.

To loaf and tweet is no great feat.

Whatever attracts attention, deserves some serious reflection.

Few are those who are not alarmingly opinionated or excessively judgmental.

We do not live by bread alone. Add a little butter!

Some accept themselves, and others suffer themselves.

We come and go with life's ebb and flow.

Yesteryear's bold gamblers are today's brash entrepreneurs.

Mankind has too many explanations for life's many inexplicables.

Wise it is to jump before you're pushed.

The strong are never wrong, and the weak are ever meek.

There is no dearth of explanations for life's inexplicables.

Too much talk makes for too little communication.

One man's work is another man's play.

Day reveals and night conceals.

To be too little aware of the present and the past, is to be too ill-prepared for the future.

The ignorant have neither intellectual ballast nor moral rudder.

Moderation has taken an extended leave of absence.

Silence is deafening and noise is troubling.

The loud are heard and heeded

Frivolity, thy name is ubiquity.

Where there's need, heed and feed.

Life has more than its fair share of steep and crooked streets.

All that comes will go, but whence and whither we will never know.

Man and woman are life's ham and eggs

Nothing is but the sum of its parts.

Reciprocity is cooperation, bargaining is confrontation.

To know oneself is but the first step in the long process of resolving one's inner problems.

Humans never change, and war never ends.

Know that thoughts beget thoughts.

Genius and insanity often walk hand in hand.

To know or understand oneself, is a trying undertaking, and subsequently to resolve one's revealed problems, is an equally agonizing challenge.

Reality will ever remain a mystery.

Education prepares for life, training prepares for a job.

Athletes are given to the body, and scholars are taken with the book.

The Gypsies and Jews are flip sides of a coin.

To know what, and to know how, will pave the way.

Manners are in order, if civility is to survive.

All is chance, all is determined, the choice is yours.

To understand is to command.

Freedom is responsibility, not licence.

Strength is power, and power uncurbed is commonly self-serving.

Insiders are snug and smug, outsiders are lean and mean.

There are child adults, and there are adult children.

The placid many accept most givens, and the restless few reject most givens.

Problems resolved, often but pose new problems.

For anarchists, chaos is the order of the day.

Milling mobs combust spontaneously.

Lies are convenient truths.

A surplus here is a dearth there. Such is life!

Mobs of angry people are as mindless and destructive as stampeding herds of animals.

To learn, one must first learn how to learn.

Politicians are more taken with politics than given to governance.

Voters know too little, and politicians do too little.

Free speech ends when lawless action is likely to begin.

Absolutes are for the bird-brained.

Pragmatists do, idealists dream.

Parents make their children after their own image.

An apple never falls far from its trunk.

Plus ça change, plus c'est la même chose:
Nero calmly fiddled while Rome burned,
The Electronics Age is blithely given to its digital game
While our warring world's ablaze.

Approaching death pales life's vanities.

Questions are spontaneous, answers are laborious.

Ours is a world more of opinions than of truths.

Leisure-time is pleasure-time.

Emoting is not to be equated with thinking.

To meet the needs and wants of the crowd, is to incite chaos.

Most of mankind's woes are of mankind's doing.

Trivia is the bliss of our Age of Electronics.

The digital world of the Electronics Age has become a blinding sandstorm more than a promised cultural oasis.

The world is a mess because humans are a mess.

When life wanes, death waxes.

One's wellbeing depends upon one's view of things.

To want ever more is to be ever discontent.

Where there is power, there is privilege.

Fear of the known disturbs, fear of the unknown devastates.

Not to pay is not to play.

Every act has consequences both good and bad.

Money is means not end.

To be different, is to be treated differently.

Foreigners are not espoused, they are exploited.

The higher the climb, the harder the fall.

Life knows no finalities.

Some have talent and others have chutzpah. The fortunate have both, and the unfortunate have neither.

Earth is what is, and heaven is what could be.

The learned think, and the wise ruminate.

Clench your fist, but throw it not.

The gifted create, the wise reflect, the thinkers think, the doers do, and most others just exist.

Unlike eating, daily cooking is more chore than taste.

Mathematics is discipline not opinion.

Christians will rejoice in Heaven, burn in Hell, or linger for some time in Limbo.

The few know, more think they know, and too many simply don't care to know.

Mental and physical competence should never cease to be extended.

The soul is but a wondrous figment of the imagination.

Awards galore are awards no more.

But for questions, there'd be no answers.

With age, nights become too short, and days become too long.

The actual is slowly yielding ground to the virtual.

Public persuasions are slowly giving ground to personal opinions.

Words can be as damaging as a physical attack.

To be what one is not, is not to be.

To forgive is not to erase, but to brush aside.

To feed one's needs and to starve one's wants, is to thrive and to survive.

To forgive, is both to demean and to elevate.

To praise another, is to attract a brother.

Women congregate, men agitate.

Women tend to be garrulous, and men are inclined to be laconic.

Women seek company, men prefer solitude.

Quality is patrician, and quantity is plebeian.

The few are burdened by their wealth, and the poor by their poverty.

The flesh is time-bound, the spirit is timeless.

To be craven is to be crafty.

A deal has its appeal.

Craft is strength.

Pragmatists and opportunists are of a kind.

To poor-mouth is to strong-arm.

Just to do no wrong, is to do too little good.

The poor of spirit are the poorest of the poor.

We come empty-handed, and we leave empty-handed.

Earth is reality, and heaven is ideality.

Humans are by far more ignorant than they are knowledgeable.

Epigrams can add a touch of poetry to mundane conversation

Elegance can be an extravagance.

Test yourself, to know yourself.

Sand, water, and sun are always fun.

To pretend to be is not to be.

Even at their best, patriotism and nationalism are but saccharine self-serving self-fictions.

Virtue is more possibility than reality.

The acceptables and unacceptables of the exceptionally gifted, characteristically differ from those of the ordinary.

The exceptional, the gifted know no rights and wrongs but theirs.

The exceptional will do the exceptional, right or wrong.

Rule breakers are society's makers and shakers.

The conventional is not for the exceptional.

Imitation is passive flattery.

Commonalities blur, differences distinguish.

Our commonalities exceed our differences.

Education begins at birth, and ends at death.

Too few voice themselves, and too many are but echoes

Serious seekers find relief in belief.

It is not meet to eat meat on Friday.

Brevity has become a necessity.

Public restlessness and impatience, make for general mayhem.

Better to flex brains than to flex muscles.

Grandiose peacetime military manoeuvres are political posturing, not military purpose.

Darkness is an absence, not a presence.

Health is a vital personal matter and a major public concern.

Acknowledge intelligence, praise hard work.

Better verbal tangle than weapon war.

Military posturing has political purpose.

Show business is make-believe and not life.

Not to be needed is not to be heeded.

The demise of a marriage is no surprise, when a marriage knows no compromise.

Not to keep adding to one's mental and physical accomplishment, is to gradually fossilize.

No birth is spared death.

Humans differ less than they are alike.

Our present world-wide messy socio-political human scene, promises an equally messy or even messier future world-wide human scene.

Human beings are no less animal than their four-legged fellow-creatures.

Religions do not explain, they but proclaim.

Language is a fluid approximation and not a fixed designation.

Not intrinsic value, but novelty and appealing appearance carry the day.

Hate speech has become more popular than civil discourse.

Do not have others do what you would not do.

Do not do unto others what you would not have others do unto you.

Both time and space are both link and separation.

Fornication is to propagation what seeding is to harvesting.

Some are dead though alive, and others are alive though dead.

To do nothing is to learn nothing.

Buy to save has become a rave.

Free speech is a slippery slope.

Terrorism not nipped in the bud, quickly becomes terrorism in the bloom.

Freedom of speech is not, and should not be an unqualified right.

Self-serving intervention invites hostility.

Force compels, persuasion invites.

Freedom of speech is a matter of idealism and realism.

Trust until there is reason to distrust.

Don't scratch when there is no itch.

Make the best of the worst, and savor the rest.

Don't eat what you cannot digest.

All is as meant to be.

Agree or disagree, but only after due reflection.

Some like it hot, some like it cold, and some just don't like it.

Life is a trying experience for one and all.

The young would be old, and the old would be young.

Civilization is of mankind's making, and reality is of unknown origin.

Civilization is drama, theater on a grand scale.

Education is a fruitful aggravation.

Tasting whets the appetite.

Squirm and worm or be a sot and rot.

Not to pay your respects to both the tangible and abstract world, is to shortchange your humanity.

One cannot reap what one has not sown.

Together, man and woman a whole do make.

Change will estrange.

We live by fiction, and die by fact.

Fictive constructs are mankind's refuge.

Fictions selectively become mankind's truths.

There are truths and there are lies, but both are in indistinguishable disguise.

Energy is as necessary for play as it is for work.

History is a messy tangle of controversial opinions.

Name-calling is not problem-solving.

Every act has consequences, good or bad or both.

Saints know sin and redemption and sinners know sin and damnation.

In heaven, there is no need for leaven.

Heaven is a beautiful fantasy, not a plausible reality.

Humans shape civilization, and civilization re-shapes humans.

All human experience is imprinted indelibly upon the brain. Unfortunately, most of these impressions are beyond retrieval.

Memory is as good as it is exercised.

It is the strong, who commonly determine what is right and wrong.

Train for a job, and educate for a profession.

The ebullient "thing culture" of the Electronics Age, has left our Western World's "human culture" in its turbulent wake.

"Things" are important, but "humans" are by far more important.

Ours has become an age of entrepreneurs and managers; the latter will create and the former will dictate, and the world will go its happy way!

Too little may be no better or no worse than too much.

Low wages spell much for few and little for many.

To silence controversy is to stoke it, not to choke it.

Unqualified patriotism is no less questionable than unqualified freedom.

Dissent tempers consent.

What was abhorred yesterday is condoned today.

The ideal is touted, the actual is lived.

Human beings are not the most loveable of god's myriad creatures.

Humans are the most creative and most destructive of earth's plethora of creatures.

Live and let live should have been God's first commandment to Adam and Eve.

Absolute rights of any sort are absolutely absurd.

In retirement, one but moves from an occupation to preoccupations.

The wealthy are healthy, and the poor are sickly.

To expand one's world of information, is to invite more reflection.

Gender once dual, today has become plural.

When robots are humanized, humans are dehumanized.

China has its opium problem, America will have its marijuana problem.

Baloney is poor fare for both body and mind.

The Hell's Angels were society's scourge.

To be absurd is to be heard.

Burp if you must, but please don't fart.

Purge, splurge and spend wisely.

Come to grips with, but not to blame.

The world of entertainment basks in frivolity and asininity.

Not to know, is to be blind.

Nothing is without meaning and purpose.

Every whole is but a small part of a vast whole.

Our world's civilization will in due time perish.
Scarred nature will then heal and flourish.

Nothing comes from nothing,
Everything comes from something!

The more the many spend, the more the few make.

Just to be, is to be too little.

Robots are being humanized, and humans are being robotized.

Team enterprise has supplanted individual achievement.

Marijuana has come of age, and will now become a rage.

Never having lived, gods never die.

Only take aboard, what you can afford.

Be quick of mind, and fleet of foot.

Take what you need, and not what you want.

Patience! There is no dearth of tomorrows.

Wants exceed needs, and needs exceed means.

Be mindful of others no less than of the self.

The laconic withdraw partially, the taciturn retreat fully.

Speak freely, but only without hate and fury.

Depression is physical lethargy and mental agony.

Be thankful for what you are, and not angry for what you are not.

Physical contact shrinks, as electronic contact swells.

Globalization has yet to change the world for the better.

Until humans change for the better, the world will remain for the worse.

Pain is both bane and gain.

Two epigrams a day, boredom will allay.

Things fall down, they don't fall up.

Teachers teach to learn.

Addictions of whatever ilk are serious afflictions.

Youth looks forward expectantly, and age looks back nostalgically.

We mouth humanity, and live inhumanity.

It is thanks to evolution that mankind still exists.

The day is obligation and exhaustion, the night is release and relief.

Live it, don't just mouth it.

Morality is more guide than club, and law is more club than guide.

Some can't sit still, and others can't get up.

Some folks are here to hear, more are here to say.

To kill is to be killed.

Bleat if you must, but only in private retreat and not in the street.

Killing should be a last resort, and not a common recourse.

To lie for a cause, is to sully that cause.

A steadfast friend is a friend indeed.

To waste today, is to want tomorrow.

Some day, every day will be a holiday.

Immigrants are strangers, and strangers have been feared, hated and maligned since time immemorial.

Humans will make robots, and robots will re-make humans.

Humans and guns spell death and destruction.

Bitters will sweeten your disposition.

Bitters are good for both mood and health.

Hypersensitivity is a relentlessly gnawing agony.

The needy are not our greedy.

Aloneness is physical, and loneliness is psychological.

Life is a wondrous maze, and a perpetual daze.

The greedy and needy are not birds of a feather.

Kill to eat, don't kill to kill.

Politicians have become more beholden to corporations than responsible to the people.

Sustainable and sustainability, have become buzz words in the business world.

To avoid risk, is to avoid life.

Life's comedy attenuates life's tragedy.

Life without risk, is cocooned survival.

The Old Testament, the New Testament and the Koran are of a kind.

Slovenly language is slovenly thought.

The eyes look, and the mind sees.

Language is a bridge that links and binds.

The ears hear, and the mind listens.

Be what you think you are, and not what others would have you be.

Think idealistically, and live pragmatically.

To pendulate between good and evil, is mankind's painful eternal lot.

Mankind is mankind's mystery of mysteries.

No one rejoices, when confronted with too many choices.

Virtue elates and sin violates.

Do not kill for pleasure or in anger.

You can be better, and can do better.

Nothing ends, but for a beginning.

To fast in protest, is pious hope at best.

Not to become a somebody, is to remain a nobody.

To be what one is not, is to be a hypocrite.

Hypocrisy is a universal tendency.

Appearance sells, and the gullible buy.

Buy and take it, should you break it.

Persons of a kind, are often of a mind.

Xenophobics, our dyed-in-the-wool haters of foreigners, are but die-hard neurotics.

Saints and sinners are the extremes of human possibility.

We are born to strive, struggle and to die.

The wise seek truth and settle for surmise.

To end in time, start in time.

For some it's dominance, for others it's submission, and for most it's just plain sex.

Glasses are not for the blind!

It's fine to drink wine, but better to drink water.

The rational feel too little,
The emotional think too little,
Better, a meld of the two.

The male is a boorish hunter, and the female a wily prey.

We talk too much about everything, and we know too little about anything.

Ignorance is bliss for some, anathema for others.

Reason and rime, each has its purpose and each has its time.

Work and play, each should have its day.

The small should stand tall, and the tall should sit down.

Race is physical, and racism is mental.

Thinkers talk little, talkers think little.

Life is an endless repetition of endless patterns.

Interest energizes, and boredom lethargizes.

Heaven is but a glorious myth of better things to come.

Work well done, is time well spent.

In friendship, men are drawn to men, and women to women.

To be efficient, is to be self-sufficient.

The truly healthy in body and mind, are hard to find.

Youth is often brash and rash, age is commonly humble and hesitant.

The ordinary many are given to the material world, the intellectual few are taken with the abstract world.

Friendships are commonly like gender.

To be self-sufficient is to be independent.

The world of sports is noted for its physical skills, not its mental prowess.

A hunter, a gun, a thrill to kill.

Some are determined to lead, and most are content to follow.

Whites are color-blinded, not color-blind.

Beauty is judgment and not attribute.

Emotions are as volatile as they are intense.

Life is the heaven or the hell each deems it to be.

A homogeneous society knows more agreement than disagreement.

For the young, change is a stimulant, for the old, tradition is a comfort.

Apostles of gloom see only doom.

The adept will prevail, and the inept will fail.

Treasure and moderate both leisure and pleasure.

Much that is popular today, will tomorrow be passé.

"Boys will be boys" is fact and excuse.

Poetry is for the few, not for the many.

When sad, weep to your heart's content.

Don't repay your enemies in kind.

Don't reach for what you can't grasp.

Eat what you should, and not what you would.

Wish for need, and not for want.

To eat to your heart's content, will leave you fat and spent.

Muscles not used, are muscles misused.

Kill if you must, and not if you will.

The strong can be assertive, the weak can be but meek.

Religious myth sustains, fiction entertains.

The human being is both the best and the worst of all God's creatures.

In distress, men tend to groan, women to weep.

Where there is life, there is strife,
Where there is strife, there is violence,
And where there is violence, there is death!

Sexual harassment is an enduring fact of life.

Give if you can, and take if you must.

Life is heaven and hell, embrace them both.

Not to suffer, is not to be alive.

Power and money are poor tokens of a person's intrinsical worth.

To accept is to make the best of life's plethora of pluses and minuses.

Blame is an all-too-common malicious game.

Dogs are to cats, what cats are to rats.

Women are treated both favorably and despicably.

Of women, mankind made a thing of beauty, and of men, mankind made a thing of brawn.

Globalism is likely to peak in an exotic meld of the Occident, the Middle East and the Orient.

Consequences make cautious.

The schooled are neither more nor less moral than the unschooled.

Pray if you will, then do what you must.

Accept thankfully in your mind, and give generously in their need.

Opposites attract, but only until the novelty wears thin.

Animals kill to live, humans live to kill.

Humans kill at will and with skill.

Not to try in fear of failure, is failure.

Those who have no choice, have no voice.

Beggars are losers, not choosers.

Romance is but a passing trance, a brief dance of chance.

A loser's plight is a finder's delight.

Not to know, is a prod to know.

Better bad parents than no parents.

Strife has become a way of life.

What is commonly right and wrong, should guide both weak and strong.

The part is no less important than the whole, and to favor one, is to neglect the other.

There is little that does not in time become passé.

The brave are idealistic, the cowards are pragmatists.

Idealists are taken with better possibility, pragmatists are given to actual consequences.

Body language often reveals, when verbal language conceals.

Thinkers go their thoughtful ways,
Idealists dream of better possibility,
Skeptics are plagued by chronic doubt,
Agnostics know nothing of certain about anything,
And nihilists are obdurate apostles of nothingness.
Such are just a few of our most prominent schools of thought.

Sins of commission are law related, and those of omission are
morals related.

Our phones are smart, their addicted users are foolish.

Christianity *wars* over religion, technology *is* our religion.

Too little change stultifies, and too much change destabilizes.

Mankind imagines, but never lives its ideal possibilities.

Ideal possibility is inspiration, not the stuff of life.

We live our drab lives, and nurture our sweet dreams.

The docile many are shaped by the willful few.

Sloppiness begins with language and hygiene.

Royalty cannot fart with impunity.

Weed is folly and greed.

Nothing is what it once was. All is flux!

To say one's say and to go one's way, is to have one's day.

Men tend to be more nature than culture.

What is marijuana but legal folly, financial greed and illusion.

What men do naturally, is not acceptable culturally.

Men are of nature roving predators.

But for sex, men and women would go separate ways.

Some pigs have but two long legs.

Mankind's motherly women have been mankind's salvation.

Human beings change rapidly, but evolve slowly.

Limits confine the male, limits protect the female.

Men tend to be sadistic, women tend to be masochistic.

The physical world is mankind's torment, and the spiritual world is its salvation.

That mankind will ever be good just to be good, is a pipe dream.

Form characterizes poetry, substance characterizes prose.

Life is an endless repetition of repetitions in ever-changing guises.

Fear of failure should not deter effort.

Not to think poetically, is not to write poetry.

An ordinary person is not a nobody.

The unheeding are often the unheeded.

The bright prevail, and the dull fail.

To have money is a bother, not to have money is a pain.

Sons adore their mothers, daughters admire their fathers.

Resistance succumbs to confidence and persistence.

Offence is often the best defence.

Parents are at their best as grandparents.

Too many people are but pose and veneer.

Calamity tries mankind's humanity.

Treat or trick, take your pick.

Too many are attracted to life's trivia, and too few are preoccupied with their human lot.

Calamity always awakens mankind's slumbering humanity.

Myths account for the unaccountable.

Perception is largely self-deception.

For most, enough is too much.

Better to please than to tease.

Action changes, activity rearranges.

Action is thought, and reaction is afterthought.

Action spurs, activity deters.

Prosecution is legality, and persecution is morality.

To persist when all goes awry, is but to wane and slowly die.

A cup half full is not a cup half empty.

Even a little help, makes a big difference.

A smile invites a smile.

Curb your appetite or your appetite will curb you.

Problems not tended to will leave you in a stew.

Plan while you still can.

Afterthought is good, forethought is better.

Not to pay on time, is to pay a fine.

To train is to prepare, to educate is to enlighten.

The dull are tedious, and the bright are devious.

Everything has its consequences, good and bad.

The best of writers distill their thoughts and condense their language.

Data has become dollars.

To ask questions is as important as to answer questions.

Transparency is a double-edged blade.

Transparency rewards everyone and spares none.

Men have their way, women have their say.

The Electronics Age is a teenage rage.

To fight for peace, is more fancy than fact.

Come to grips and to terms with the self, and then with life itself.

One's IQ is more interpretation than estimation.

Force is always a bad recourse.

Better to aid than to upbraid.

Not to be at peace with the self, is to be at odds with others.

To robotize is to dehumanize.

Judeo-Christianity once spiritualized western culture, the Electronics Age has today thingmatized it.

'Tis not meet to cheat.

The fleet of mind are often slow of foot.

A frown is a silent put-down.

Smiles attract and grimaces distract.

Actuality, not virtuality, is our reality.

God creates, and man but makes.

God is as flawed as his human creations.

The devil is but an angel gone astray.

The universe is a whole that ever evolves but essentially never changes.

Planet Earth is never more and never less.

Know the past, to shape the future.

People here or there, are basically the same.

The Electronics Age has changed the face of the whole world.

America's touted upward social mobility has become a disturbing downward slide.

Politics is party-minded, legislation is people-minded.

Interdependence is more fulfilling than independence.

Nihilism is born of embittered idealism.

Civilization is nature's ruination.

One person's addiction is every person's affliction.

Knowing obligates doing.

One person's love is another person's hate.

Digitalia's happy merry-go-round will eventually become a trying roller coaster.

Things are not unimportant, but it's best to invest in humans.

Contentment is a mental high, happiness is an emotional high.

Constantly to question, is constantly to quarrel.

Mountains of good will are humanly more salutary than mountains of cash.

A country's financial wellbeing depends no less upon its human capital than upon its economic capital.

No human is this or that, but rather, this and that and whatever else.

Government has become more politics than governance.

Trumpian New Age Politics is all bombast and skullduggery.

Unadulterated freedom demands as much as it gives.

Financial literacy has become vastly more important than cultural literacy.

Men in power, women deflower.

Plumb your joys and plumb your woes, for they are the very stuff of life.

Depression and elation are flip sides of the same coin.

The longer the exercise, the stronger the muscle.

Morality demands and rewards.

But for earth, water, air and fire, there'd be no life.

Do your thing and go your way, but do know too, that there's a price to pay.

Would that humans were what they should be.

Too much for the few leaves too little for the many.

To school is to educate, to train, and to socialize.

Purge the male of his unruly sexual urge.

The sexual urge knows no right or wrong.

To ask sensitive questions, is to be told blatant lies.

A serious question deserves an honest answer.

A courteous "Thank you" invites a friendly "You're welcome."

Take to task if you must, but be brief and just.

Don't just bitch, scratch your itch.

When the fuse is lit, don't just sit.

It's no fun to be on the run.

To make ends meet, spendthrifts need but spend less.

When things go awry, stiffen your lips, don't cry.

Rain quenches Mother Earth's thirst.

When the chips are down, don't leave, stick around.

Be seriously pensive in thought and not desperately defensive.

The hoity-toities think they know, and the hoi polloi wish they knew.

It is not enough to wish, it's imperative to fish.

Robots will soon do most of what humans presently do.

Mankind's restless curiosity and imaginative creativity, guarantee constant cultural drifts.

Many swim, more just float.

Do your vigorous best, and then relax content and rest.

Needs should get attention, wants but mention.

The hoi polloi are pigs and the hoity-toities are prigs.

To try to disabuse a non-thinking ignoramus of untenable convictions, is an exercise in futility.

The fat would be leaner, and the lean would be fatter.

To be downright upright, is not a contradiction.

To feel for, is to feel better.

To pity is good, to help is better.

Women choose to sit, and men prefer to flit.

Polygamy's for the male, and monogamy's for the female.

To have a choice, is to have a voice.

Better a racing mind and pacing body, than a pacing mind and a racing body.

Women want their home, men prefer to roam.

A setback may deflate, but can also invigorate.

Do it or rue it!

To eat to one's heart's content , is to become fat and rent.

An alarmingly large number of people today are quite unmarketable.

Today's dream will become tomorrow's realities.

Americans are too busy to listen.

America gives liberally, but takes greedily.

Women tend to intuit, men prefer to reason.

Education begins at birth, and should continue until death.

Children shout and play, adults talk and toil.

We embrace too readily, and reject too readily.

Discard and accumulate more discreetly and moderately.

The latest is not necessarily the best.

Buyers are seduced by novelty, and not by usefulness or quality.

The old cling to the bygone, the young embrace the new.

Things are never what people would have them be.

Multiculturalism quickly becomes cultural chaos.

The few indulge in their much, and the many languish in their little.

Many of the few will be memorialized, but few of the many will be remembered.

The wealthy look forward to their more of tomorrow, and the poor look forward to their next meal.

A mold of the feeler, thinker and doer, would augur well for society.

A chance spurt and inert mass became organic mess.

Words are a plenitude of diverse building blocks creatively juxtaposed by the few, and awkwardly arranged by the many.

The dead are life's best guides.

It is not enough but to breathe and move.

The cheery amuse, the dour confuse.

We talk too much and do too little.

Men overpower and women undermine.

The asocial have become common and brazen, the dwindling socially upright have become angry and given to fight.

Men prevail and women quail.

Men do women and women undo men.

No idea is uncontested.

'Tis good to rest after you have done your best.

Don't wallow in muck, swim in thought.

Modesty is a virtue, a virtue that will hurt you.

The good casts little light, sin alone glows bright.

Virtue shines, and sin blinds.

Don't wring your hands, use them.

Some worm and squirm, others thrash and flail.

There is always another point of view.

Hew to the line or rue the day.

Freedom unqualified invites licence, and licence spells chaos.

The American Dream has lost its gleam.

Education sharpens minds, training sharpens skills.

A touch of humility promotes civility.

The self-righteous upright are downright obnoxious.

Too many are emotionally too volatile or too fixed in their thinking.

Failure distresses, and success impresses.

Both failure and success are contagious.

The willing are not always the able.

Managers manage and workers work.

Some, though present, are absent, others, though absent, are present.

Some think and do, and too many do neither.

Work and play should in balance interplay.

There should be no room for either despair or gloom.

The hale and hearty are steady guests at every party.

Too many politicians are small-minded though big-headed.

Women have been harassed since time immemorial. Change is overdue!

Headless drivers are probably more dangerous than driverless cars.

Be of good cheer, Christmas shopping is here.

Age alone a sage does not make.

To be a scholar is good, to be a scholar and a decent human being is better.

The school shapes mentally, the family shapes morally.

In choice, quality is imperative, diversity is desirable.

The labor of the many fills the coffers of the few.

Outer self will lure, inner self will secure.

Appearance *will* draw attention, substance *should* determine intentions.

Beauty *will* wane, but mind *can* gain.

Dine fine, think sharp.

Dream when asleep, and think when awake.

We see what we want to see, and do what we should not do.

Euphoria knows too little sobriety.

For some, work is an end in itself, for most others, work is but a means to an end.

The appalling excesses of the Electronics Age will soon become galling.

Too many people are less than they could be.

He barks and she meows, and ne'er the twain will meet.

Be cautious, don't reveal until you've made a deal.

Too many are but jetsam and flotsam on the sea of life.

Though ever changing, each is ever the same.

Better to try and fail than to fail to try.

To be sorry is good, to be sorry and to atone is better.

Too many do little more than sleepwalk their way through life.

Death, like life, is omnipresent.

Birth is a becoming, and death an unbecoming.

But for life there would be no death, and but for death, there would be no life.

Life and death walk hand in hand.

Too many don't know enough to know, that they don't know enough.

Many are much more than they think they are.

Self-esteem and self-confidence make for smooth sailing.

Many are much less than they think they are.

Addressed aggressively, wanting self-esteem and self-confidence will shrink progressively.

God created Adam and Eve, then left them to their own devices.

Do not let your jollies become your follies.

Gods create, humans propagate.

We elect and nominate, to let others dominate.

The bad is natural, the good is cultural.

Brains and brawn are salt and pepper.

Earth is a reality, and heaven is a possibility.

Heaven and earth are flip sides of the same coin.

Every decision has its pros and cons.

Life is strife and battle, not brotherhood and peace.

Humble prayer can make the unacceptable acceptable.

Don't reach for, beseech more.

To be kind, is to be of a rare kind.

To flaunt one's wares, is but to attract envious stares.

The battle is not won, until the enemy is on the run.

A modicum of pride goes a long way.

Health makes for wealth, and wealth makes for health.

Our poor in spirit are our poorest.

Our religious institutions are no better, and also no worse, than society's other sundry institutions.

People of a mind, one another quickly find.

Slaves have been a common cultural commodity since time immemorial.

Every culture has had its hoity-toities and its hoi polloi.

To make cannabis legal and recreational, is to sow the seed and to reap the whirlwind.

Women have their share of masochists, and men, their share of sadists.

The blacks play, the whites pay, and the sports world rumbles on.

Football will eventually injure itself to death.

When people become estranged—as in our Electronics Age—culture will wane.

Where brawn is imperative, blacks put whites to shame, where brain is imperative, whites put blacks to shame.

Too many lawmakers have also become lawbreakers.

In high places, licence has almost become a privilege.

Men do what they do, because they are what they are.

Men are sexually driven, and morally riven.

Women, though reluctantly, have always suffered man's obnoxious normalities.

We are but creatures of a jungle driven by our own needs and wants.

To be kind is to foster kindness.

Morality condones more than it stifles.

Women are intrinsically more accommodating than men.

Would that the give and take of life were balanced.

Sleep is respite and recovery.

Use the brain to common gain.

Stealth is a shortcut to wealth.

When day is spent and you are rent, it's best to rest.

Immorality is, immediately, more rewarding than morality.

Men are stronger, but women live longer.

A carriage, a marriage and a cottage, what more would you want!

Egality, fraternity and liberty have served the French right well and long.

Royalty has become an anachronism.

Politics once quite avocational, has become progressively more vocational.

Universities, once monastic, have become part of the marketplace.

Obstacles are here to be overcome, and not to overcome.

To forget the past, is to be confronted by the present.

To scream is a reaction, not a response.

Humility is more utility than futility.

Absolutists know no compromise.

Each is a unique composite of action, feeling, thought, imagination, values, beliefs and skills.

Sexual congress is ardent, anxious and fraught with friction.

President Trump is, to an alarming degree, a typical American.

Religions in jeopardy, lose their humanity.

Where there are deadly weapons, there will be violent deaths.

To eat too much and to exercise too little, has its inevitable consequences.

Technology's plethora of electronic devices both unburdens and burdens.

Cyberaddiction has become a widespread affliction.

Political sanctions are as effective as slaps on the wrist.

Truths are not facts, and facts are not truths.

Absolutists have no truck with compromise.

Ideally, justice is only served when justice is dispensed.

Verify facts and dignify truths.

Don't leave undone what you've begun.

To learn too little and to forget too much, is a common malady.

Novelties are very distracting attractions.

Digital devices and games have supplanted books and thought.

Too many of the exuberant billionaires of our manic Electronics Age, are King Turds on Shit Island.

Would that our Electronics Age were more given to humans and less taken with things.

For the few, the many are but means, not ends.

Civilization and culture are of mankind, all else is of unknown origin.

What we are, and why we are what we are and what we will become, is beyond human ken.

Mankind, in its quest for truth, cannot go beyond informed opinion.

We would be gods, and are but opinionated mortals.

It is only in their dreams and imagination, that mortals become like gods.

Life is a constant becoming and unbecoming.

More of the same does not change the game.

To hurry too much, is to tarry too little.

There is much good, but even more evil in most of us.

While adults are given to their vices, children are often left to their own devices.

Yesteryear's art of letter-writing has become today's puny tweets and lean E-mail.

The Industrial Revolution transformed society, and Artificial Intelligence will soon transfigure it.

Bookshelves are becoming collector items.

Skills have begun to languish, and digital devices to flourish.

One is, to an alarming degree, what one does.

Quality is appreciated, but quantity sells.

Ill manners and sloppy dress betoken cultural stress.

Sexual harassment is an ugly existential reality.

Might is right, but only when it's not wrong.

Where there's no scrutiny, there should be mutiny.

The plethora of perplexing acronyms and cute neologisms of the Electronics Age, is more confusing than amusing.

Do not repair or replace what is not broken.

New England of old had its witches to scold.

Mankind has its rare exceptionals, those head and shoulders above all others.

Genius is a meld of nature and culture.

Farmers give us bread and butter, entrepreneurs give us apps and gadgets.

To husband is to have a tomorrow.

Sexual harassers have had their day, and now society will have its say.

One wrong righted, is often also another right wronged.

Life is a bundle of countless paradoxes.

Female gall and guile have always managed to manage male chauvinism.

Some would argue straight-faced, that the wealthy invest their money, and the poor squander theirs on booze and women.

Cultivate virtue, and counter vice.

Where cats abound, mice are rarely around.

To strive for the unattainable, is laudable.

Just to patiently wait for fortune's smile, is rarely worth one's while.

To focus on the self, is not to see the other.

The unreal has begun to supplant the real.

From farm to factory to digitalia: A wondrous cultural evolution?

Exercise kindness and exorcize malice.

Language is the bond that binds as does no other.

But for earth, water, fire and air, our planet would be cold and bare.

Freedom is most appreciated in its loss.

To live yourself, is to learn to know yourself.

Do your will, but reflect both before and after, before you do.

To believe but what has been instilled, is to shortchange the self.

To kill is easier, when the enemy's first been demonized.

To imprison is to discard, to rehabilitate is to salvage.

Prisons are expensive, prison farms and factories can be self-sufficient.

To punish in the present, what was tolerated or acceptable in the past, is a dangerous precedent.

Power has always enjoyed privilege and licence.

To focus and to punish the male's past sexual harassment of women is good, and to prevent present and future sexual violation of women is even better.

Much condoned today, will be condemned tomorrow.

Leaders make war at the expense of their people.

Attractions are distractions, and distractions are attractions.

Boredom is a psychological response to too much or too little stimulation.

To pay attention to detail, is to succeed and not to fail.

Focus and tenacity enhance capacity.

Digital distraction compromises traction.

Take care of your mind, and your mind will take care of your body.

Diminished activity, mental or physical, diminishes the focus and attention span.

A life without purpose, is a life without meaning.

We are not here but to fill space.

We should know better than to think that we know.

Friends are here to help and to be helped.

Pent-up anger is a waste of energy.

With every new death, the dead of old die anew.

Our healthiest are our wealthiest.

Regret is a reaction, not a solution.

To be someone you must first become someone.

Better to spend money saved, than money not yet earned.

A good day's work deserves a good day's pay.

Honest effort is laudable regardless of result.

Think much, and say little.

To cheat is never meet.

The tough are never meek, and the meek are never tough.

Orgasm's purpose is procreation and not recreation.

More can be less, and less can be more.

Sometimes it's best just to sit and rest.

But for change, time would be timelessness, and multiplicity would be oneness.

In mental growth, old fictions are shed for new.

To remember past mistakes, is to reduce future blunders.

What was ignored yesterday, is deplored today.

Lying should be last resort, not a ready means.

In learning, we discard and add, and hope for the best.

Every culture has had its god or gods. Like it or not!

A child needs its parent, a culture needs its god.

Take heart, time is a timeless placebo.

Chide yourself, but even better, change yourself.

The more one knows, the more one rejoices and agonizes.

To be bridled, is to bristle.

To be free, is to culturally go astray.

Decisions and actions leave one distraught, but for fore- and afterthought.

All too few human beings worm and squirm as best they can, and all too many are just a presence.

Our planet was once a world out of joint, it has become an inferno whose days are numbered.

Each is but a passing presence, not a monument.

Time should be husbanded and not squandered.

Woman, no longer willing to be but a presence in the shadow of the male, is determined to cast her own shadow.

Civilization brainwashes its people, and scars the face of the earth.

We have known for a long time that our world is a round sphere, but our eyes would continue to have it be an endless flat plain.

Be other-minded, if you must, but also open-minded, if you can.

Heed and do, but not before you've thought it through.

Women would do well to mother, rather than smother their sons.

Pursue your cause passionately, but reflectively and with pause.

Thought is born of need, interest and curiosity.

Better to mother than to smother.

Cultivate, and moderate feelings.

Husband provides, and wife presides.

It pays off to show off.

Were each what each would or should be, the world a better place would be.

Everything is a consequence, and has its consequences.

Aggressive masculinity has long been a worldwide bane. It's time to purge this scourge.

Number makes a difference in relationships: The fewer the more intimate, the more, the less personal.

For man, woman is the unknown other, and for woman, man is the unknown other.

Moderation should be one's vocation.

Humans, naturally social beings, are simultaneously willfully independent: A trying lot.

The good are never as good as they seem to be, and the bad are never as bad as deemed to be.

Neither wealth nor poverty are gauges of human worth.

We came from erewhon, and will leave for erewhon.

It's better to have than not to have, but it's even better to give.

It would be good if women were more woman, and men were less man.

Robots are toys for the big boys.

Digital mania will in due time pale, and interest will again shift from things to human beings.

Goodness for the sake of goodness, is still a pipe dream.

Each culture, like every day, is something old and something new.

Use it or lose it, is not an idle adage.

When truth pales, all else fails.

For some, religion is joyous celebration, and for many others, it is pure desperation.

A drone, once but a sophisticated toy for a playful boy, quickly became a deadly weapon for a soldier-boy: An appalling misuse and abuse.

Digitalized technology has both transfigured and disfigured society.

The digital age is humanizing things, and thingmatizing humans.

Things have become an attraction, and humans, a distraction.

A business must grow, and not just be: The business world's insanity!

Sexual harassment long tolerated, may at long last be terminated.

Dying words: So be it, if it must so be.

The adage, live and let live, is but honored in its breech.

Just to sit, will lethargize, not energize.

To be depressed, is to be profoundly at odds with the self and with life at large.

To know good is good, to do good is better.

Individually we are of but short duration, life, on the other hand, is a timeless continuum.

Many of yesteryear's virtues have today become questionable, many of yesterday's sins have today become quite acceptable.

Cannabis, once damned and illegal, has become society's latest passionately-embraced panacea. There's gold in them thar hills!

In the throes of waned cultural dissolution, both Islam and Christianity have passed the point of no return.

The essence of religion is ecstasy and not rationality.

Decency has become a casualty.

Accidental conception invites deliberate rejection.

Unwed mothers, once looked at askance, now don't get a second glance.

Some run because it is fun, many others run because they are on the run.

Digital labor is for today, what manual labor was for yesterday.

In sport, the Blacks perform and the Whites observe.

The world indulges in war, and talks about peace.

Eating whets the appetite.

To be different is not to be inferior.

Sexual thrill can lead to kill.

For women, men are a desirable necessity and an annoying presence.

Take care of your body, and it will take care of you.

The world of apps and devices has supplanted the world of letters.

It is good to evolve *thinking things*, but it is better to improve *thinking minds*.

Things are programmed, humans think.

All that is, is all that ever was, and all that will ever be.

Something created all that is, and then left everything to its own devices.

To reap, one must first sow.

Sex is a meld of elation and vexation.

Trust invites cooperation, distrust invites confrontation.

The plethora of expensive quirky home gadgets, is more ingenious novelty than pressing necessity.

Don't speak or do before you think.

High heels are loud and sassy, low heels are mum and glum.

Too many intellectuals are content just to be passively discontent.

Faith is belief where reason doubts.

You and life are what you make of them.

Gods have their truths, and humans live their fictions.

But few know enough to know that they don't know enough.

We come and we go, from where and to where, we do not know.

The Judeo-Christian culture is old, worn and torn, and the worst is yet to come.

Verbal battles too often become weapon wars.

The unsolicited popo-pinch that delights the young wench, is very likely to startle and anger the staid matron.

To be ignored is to be reduced.

Male glances of genuine admiration are appreciated by all women, and some even take fleeting delight in the passing lascivious male stare.

Stare if you will or must, but don't touch!

Pragmatism and expediency are of this world, and idealism is but dream and fantasy. So some do claim!

The rhetoric of hate is tempting bait.

Differences must be transcended, if wars are ever to be ended.

Being is becoming, and ever more bewildering.

Opt for aloneness and thoughtfulness, rather than for noisy crowd and blather.

Humans are animals, and animals behave like animals.

Beliefs not lived are living lies.

Concern not exercised, is indifference in disguise.

Break bread with those who have none.

Difference should be appreciated, not hated.

Sport should be more display of skills, and less determination to win.

Government and politics are birds of a different feather.

Virtues are generally and loudly acclaimed, only quickly and all too often to be disclaimed.

We gain and we lose, whenever we choose.

If fast, you will last, and if slow, you will go.

When in doubt, reject don't accept.

The malevolent scheme, and the benevolent dream.

Jews, Christians, and Muslims are but variations on a theme.

The Electronics Age is intent upon improvement and not upon explanation.

Metaphysics tried to explain, technology is determined to improve.

Church, the guardian of religion, has always been laudable.
Church, the politicized institution, has always been questionable.

Redemption merits forgiveness.

Accept life for all its pluses and minuses, and make the best of it.

Most people get from life what they give to life.

Society is morality-minded, the jungle is survival-minded.

Grin and bear it, or tear your hair and scream. Yours is the choice!

It is not enough just to be alive.

To be blind to detail, is to do and fail.

Education sophisticates, training remunerates.

Life without pain, is loss not gain.

Reality is a complexity that will always be beyond human accountability.

Advantage should never have become privilege, and privilege should never have become licence.

Had men and women become more appreciatively mindful of their intrinsic differences, they would never have used and abused each other to the degree that they do.

Be mindful of the other, embrace the other, for the other is your brother, differences notwithstanding.

Differences commonly agitate and rouse hostility, but they can, and do, also attract, stimulate and enrich.

Children will be children, and many adults are not much different.

The done cannot be undone!

Younger women opt for revealing dress, and older women prefer appealing apparels.

One is socially in and of, when hand fits glove.

For the happy child, the world is a delightful fairyland, and for the stressed adult, the world is a trying labor camp.

Improve we can, change we can't.

To love it, you must be in it and of it.

Form is thought and thought is form.

It's never as bad as it seems to be.

Our tomorrows are born in our todays.

To refine your language and distill your thought, will surely improve your lot.

To venture is both pain and gain.

We do to learn, and we learn to do.

Belief consoles, and myth extols.

To be more and more connected electronically, is to be less and less connected humanly.

Electronic apps lethargize as readily as they energize.

The Digital World has been as compelling as it is accommodating.

Electronic possessions have become obsessions.

Electronic engagement is good, but human interaction is better.

Decent human beings are not a dime a dozen.

Silence can be very telling.

Men violate and women manipulate.

Tit for tat, is give and take.

Men venerate and violate, and women mother and manipulate.

Our somebodies are few, our nobodies are many.

To be *in it*, one must be, or become *of it*.

Difference annoys as much as it attracts.

Civilization and nature are testy bedmates.

For men, sex is drive, and for women, sex is drive and want.

What folly, television's fare!

Time alone does not solve problems.

Excessive analysis results in paralysis.

Immoral means never achieve moral ends.

Blood is red, no matter what color the skin.

Only non-violence will ever achieve the peace and justice that have eluded violence.

To change the whole, start with the part.

You can't take off your socks, before you've removed your shoes.

To talk too much is to hear too little.

Ad hominems are fire fuel, not fire extinguishers.

To engage in folly, is to be a fool.

Tin cans kicked down the street, don't dissolve in the rain.

Sucklings learn early in life, that effort is rewarding.

To be independent, is to be free.

To be bereft of humanity, is to be truly poverty-stricken.

All of mankind's gods and devils, have been within and not without.

Religions are a blessing, and religious institutions are a curse.

Nature creates, and civilization shapes.

Decency is an optional human possibility.

To expose and punish, should be less restrictive and more rehabilitative.

Possessions are blessing and burden.

The monetary ranking of humans is rank.

Together, children and puppies are a blessing and outright joy.

Cherish, don't disparage the other.

Strength and love together, are better than strength and love apart.

Acknowledgement elevates, condescension denigrates.

Adults hyperbolize, children fantasize.

The male wants to do, and the female prefers to be done.

The never known can never be forgotten.

The "dos" and "don'ts" are compelling, the "oughts" and the "ought nots" are inviting.

The pangs of birth and the throes of death, are every culture's givens.

Each is a human being, not a human thing.

Prophets are as good as they are persuasive.

A prophet unheard, is but a voice in the wilderness.

Unfettered freedom is bane not gain.

To get along, one need but go along.

One is not *of* and *in*, to the degree that one is different.

To try and to fail, is both to gain and to lose.

To have failed, is to have tried and learned.

Chance is ignorance or evasion, not explanation.

People, rich or poor, are equally good or bad.

Change is not without its causes and purposes.

None of mankind's physical attributes have been without purpose.

The living evolve with life's circumstances.

Anything that does everything, is not likely to do anything well.

Some are given to life, others are taken with death, and many just *are*.

Boys will be boys, and girls *would be* boys. Or so it seems!

Once the blush is off the bloom, joy will quickly turn to gloom.

Little craves and much cloys.

Appearance seems, and substance tells.

The gods know, humans want to know.

Victims blame, and victors acclaim.

The gifted are *few,* the *would-bes* are many.

There are the pushers and the pushed. And both are to be blamed.

Thought gives and takes.

Thought can be enhanced by feeling, and feeling by thought.

Correction may improve, punishment will harden.

Opinion holds dominion.

Teachers and students are both students and teachers.

Thoughts fertilize thinking.

To be in control, is to be out of control.

The human community is a hotbed of absurdity.

Truths are rewarding, but also take their toll.

Lies irritate, but also lubricate.

Even little lies can have big consequences.

Trust you must, if you cherish your marriage.

Some are strong both physically and mentally. The fortunates!
Others are weak both physically and mentally. The unfortunates!
And still others are a mixture of strength and weakness. The
ordinary!

Brains are inherited, minds are cultivated.

The unfortunates of life are no less worthy of appreciation and respect than life's fortunates.

Not to report abusive sexual behavior, is to abet it.

Whistle-blowers should be commended, not upended.

Life has more than just its few winners and many losers.

Optimists do something to achieve, pessimists do nothing for fear of failure.

Optimism involves, and pessimism disengages.

To listen thoughtfully is to engage meaningfully.

Many questions are more reprimand than query.

Solutions often spawn new problems.

Busywork is purposeful but empty display.

To be strong physically is good, to be strong psychologically is better.

Both work and play are enhanced by purpose.

For the workaholic, to work is no less necessary than to breathe.

To want to know, is to want to grow.

Morality discriminates, expediency motivates.

Thieves take, and their victims are taken.

Ever to take to task and ever to yearn for something better, is to be ever blind to both self and life.

The faceless many have always been duped and exploited by the powerful few.

Cryptomoney is funny money.

America, a country of peace, is ever at war.

A promise is but a beginning.

The new attracts, the old distracts.

Times do change!
Why work? The answer was: To make a living.
Why work? The answer is: To make a fortune.

Children are playful, the old are woeful.

Some think that work is for others.

To tell how to do is good, but to show how to do is better.

Self-knowledge and self-realization should be common aspirations.

Propensity gives life direction and intensity.

Money will be made, however, whenever, and wherever money can be made.

Newspapers feature life's many wrongs at the expense of life's many rights.

Educate for life, and train for jobs.

To spell English correctly, is a challenge for the best of writers.

Walls that enclose, assure quiet and repose.

To understand, is to be in command.

Trivia and lies are never a surprise.

Children look to the future, the old are given to the past.

Data should assist and not determine.

Our sun neither rises nor sets, all but revolves about it.

Lest it be forgotten!
The humanities are an incredible complement to any field of study.

Scientific truths are result, political truths are purpose.

Paths invite, and streets oblige.

Boys and girls are reality, lads and maidens are ideality.

Hidden paths stir idle curiosity; highways spell speed and purpose.

Effort rewards, sloth invites.

Statistics suggest, don't tell.

For the many, the Stock Market is more gamble than informed investment.

Compulsion compels, caution constrains.

For all too many, life is more nightmare than dream.

What goes up, will come down.

Digital life is not here to stay; by who knows when, it will be yesterday.

Profanities are inanities.

Better to have little surprises than big expectations.

Human beings will never cease to exploit the exploitable.

Incarceration without rehabilitation, is nothing less than mindlessness.

Children laugh and play, the old frown and pray.

When no longer in and of, it's then time to grieve and leave.

Law impinges upon freedom, and freedom impinges upon law.

Sexual harassment has loosed the hounds of both vengeance and justice.

That life ever changes, is indisputable.
That it ever changes for the better, is debatable.

Simply to dismiss the controversial opinions of others, is to remain mired in one's own.

Mankind has been as destructive as it has been constructive.

Mankind's eventual undoing will probably be of its own doing.

When there is no compromise, there is no agreement.

Multiculturalism and racial and ethnic diversity are a formidable challenge for Democracy.

Constants are few in life's fickle flow of change.

The dance of chance is more jitterbug than waltz.

To be obliging is to become obliged.

Where there is no choice, there is no voice.

When there's too much choice, people cease to choose.

To have everything, is to appreciate nothing.

We learn to learn by learning.

The bad is always noted, the good is often ignored.

Aloneness is physical, loneliness is psychological.

Too many eat too much, and too few eat enough.

All pumps have to be primed.

A boy is a joy, a girl is a pearl.

Proverbs are old friends, epigrams are more recent acquaintances.

To learn is to know, to guess is to gamble.

Winners and losers should be friends, not foes.

Actresses and actors become what they are not.

War should be a last recourse, and not a first response to evolving differences.

Reflection makes for correction and new direction.

Dolce far niente, or how sweet it is just to sit and stare.

The lazy are cunning, and not crazy.

Romantic love is frantic love.

Retribution is not a solution.

Life's passion is continued life.

Women are most at home with women, and men are most at home with men.

Not to seek, is clearly not to find.

When memory fails, life pales.

Infatuation is nothing more than brief emotional intoxication.

A lover is a thrill, a companion is a comfort.

Rest is as necessary and as rewarding as work.

To educate is to humanize, to train is to robotize.

Dehumanization is as common as it is profitable.

To train and not to educate is to dehumanize.

Lower-class Blacks were once robotized to serve the purposes of the plantation world.
Middle-class workers of today are being robotized to serve the purposes of our corporate world.
Variations on an old theme!

Mankind's genius has been both blessing and curse.

Men aspire to, women long for!

The military is less brain than muscle.

Surfeit cloys, while enough buoys.

The conventional and the predictable are social pacifiers.

Erase what can and should be erased, and let the indelible be.

To long for ever more, is never to be content.

Differences lead to quarrels, and quarrels end in violence, and all is as it has always been.

The robotizing of humans, and the humanizing of robots, is mankind's latest fantasizing.

Smart phones should not be toys for little girls and little boys.

Intelligence is potential that manifests itself in skills.

To be somebody or to be a nobody, that is the question!

The Western World's Judeo-Christian culture has taken wing, and the Electronics Age's plethora of trivial devices and apps has settled in.

Culturally, America is regressing, not progressing. The end is nigh!

Changed we have, and change we will until we're stiff and still.

The *human condition* is beyond cognition.

Action not prefaced by thought, is likely to come to nought.

Populism cultivates popular fictions.

Don't invent what you don't need.

That human beings are never as free as they want to be, is a blessing.

The content do not have to wish.

Freedom unqualified by responsibility, is licence.

Outer beauty attracts, inner beauty binds.

The bold will venture forth, the timid will shy away.

Freedom is ideality not reality.

The old is habit and the new is challenge.

Every life is an evolving novel.

If all were wealthy, there would be no poor.

Life is strife and struggle, both debilitating and exhilarating.

Hunger is a wrenching food-focussed drive that ironically both overwhelms appetite and dulls the taste buds.

The poor are poor because of the rich,
And the rich are rich because of the poor.
Such simplistic equations as these,
Are no more than frivolous tease.

Our digital age of communication, has made matter of idle chatter.

Activity is not action, nor is loquacity conversation.

To shout, is not to sing, nor is to shuffle about, to dance.

A house can become a home, and a yard can become a garden.

According to our financial world: To grow is to flourish, and not to grow is to perish.

Political purges are too often more scourge than purge.

Better to prevent than to cure.

Don't rant and flog, chant and pray.

Prevention deters absolutely, punishment deters relatively.

Populism is pollution, not solution.

America, once laudable, has become right laughable.

What is good for thee, may not be good for me.

Youth is given to becoming, and age is taken with being.

We recall the past, focus on the present, and prepare for the future.

The few lead, the many follow, and ne'er the twain will meet.

Tomorrow will be of today's doing, just as today is of yesterday's doing.

Blame, not change, is the name of the game.

The politically-correct is characteristically less wise than ill-advised.

Heed your speed or end in need.

Tend to today, and plan for tomorrow.

Failures and successes are not finalities, and each life has its share of both.

Self-appreciation is no less suspect than other-appreciation.

The world is out of joint, because humans are out of joint.

Sins of omission are no less sinful than sins of commission.

Reason, rather than emote to promote.

To work or to play is to be active, and to be active is to be alive.

The more mature, the more responsibility.

Hypersensitivity is both blessing and curse.

When our mythic black-caped messenger with scythe appears, another human disappears.

America is right, even when America is wrong.

To admit a weakness, is to be strong.

Populism knows without knowing.

Anti-intellectualism is at the very heart of America's *modus operandi.*

A popular misconception: to know is to impede both decision and action.

Think then do, then think anew.

To think more is to do better.

To be given to things, is to become a thing.

To add to your things, is not to add to your person.

Resolve to evolve and not to dissolve.

Too little action and too much thought, is very likely to leave you distraught.

Attractions quickly become distractions.

To think is to know, and to know is to grow.

To understand, is to forgive.

Being can become a tumultuous becoming.

One gets nothing for nothing.

Tether passion and let compassion range.

Up and to it, or you will rue it.

Democracies are inclined to become slopocracies.

Humans have harassed each other since time immemorial.

Pay your debts, or pay the consequences.

Procrastination moves, it does not remove.

The bold take a hold, the timid withhold.

Thoughts are reflective and feelings are reflexive.

Birth is chance and death is fate.

Some just live life, and some just ponder life.

Thought is for the cerebral, and action is for the physical.

Oh, that moments of bliss would but tarry awhile!

Digitalia's gadgetry has been a tasteless waste of talent and time.

Peace has become but a restive lull in warfare.

Today's harassed become tomorrow's harassers.

Religion is essentially firm belief in better possibility.

Mental maturity is more elusive than physical maturity.

Belated thought is better than no thought.

Time heals, death ends.

Statistics do not conclude, they inform.

Absolutes are absolutely absurd.

Certainty is at best but informed reaction.

Brawn reduces and brain seduces.

Beauty is much more than but skin-deep.

Thoughts excite, feelings overwhelm.

Thought without language is action without movement.

Weigh circumstances, obey morality.

To talk just to talk, is to say nothing.

All is planned or all is chance.

Mankind's dos and don'ts don't change with its changing beliefs.

Life's imponderables will never cease to plague mankind.

When impulse prevails, order fails.

Power breeds corruption.

In the World of Finance, morality's straight and narrow path quickly becomes a broad and crooked freeway.

Privilege easily becomes licence, and licence quickly becomes corruption.

Civilization is intrinsically unnatural, ergo, essentially at odds with the natural world.

Change we do, and change we will.

It is fun to have fun.

You will rue, what you should but do not do.

To persuade is better than to bribe.

Expectation courts disappointment.

In going controversy, either party can end it, but neither party does.

Men take, women bait.

The higher the climb, the harder the fall.

Mankind would deem itself God's *chef d'oeuvre*!

Our earth and its life are a mystery that will remain a mystery.

Sex is life's generator.

Without sex, life would be very lifeless.

To be used is to be abused.

To know little of the self, is to be ignorant of others.

Prayers are more request than thanks.

Better to propose than to dispose.

In spite of, and because of!

Work wears, rest repairs.

Life is death's price.

Goodness bores and lethargizes, the questionable attracts and energizes.

Lies travel faster than do truths.

Corruption is a ubiquitous seduction.

Time and space are the universe's major invisible phenomena, phenomena rendered measurable by reality's perpetual becoming.

To be is to be flawed!

To transgress is to regress.

We live by fiction, not by bread alone.

Life is suffering and death is oblivion.

Earth is mankind's temporary abode, Heaven is its permanent home.

Idealists are dreamers, and pragmatists are schemers.

Activity, both physical and mental, make for health, both physical and mental.

A healthy brain promotes a healthy mind.

To have nothing to say, is to waste away.

Contrition is an admission of some violation.

To thrash and flail is not to fail.

The young would be old, and the old would be young.

Why is what is, what it is?

Earth is hell, and Heaven is fiction.

Practice does not perfect, it only improves.

Would that the hardly thought, were already wrought.

Blame is a game that both punishes and rewards.

To know the unknowable is a peculiar human madness.

Ours is an intimate relationship with sod!
We are first temporarily above it,
And then permanently below it.

Every start demands some ken and takes some heart.

Even a small change can make a big difference.

We hope to know, and know we never will.

To know does not solve, but it does comfort.

Wants exceed needs.

The past is an atlas, the future but a relief map.

To know too much, is to do too little.

Money does for you, what you do for money.

For most Whites, Blacks were once lesser human beings, and for many Whites today, they still are.

When opponents are intransigent, and when dialogue is impossible, violence becomes inevitable.

Reality is as inscrutable as it is intriguing.

One learns much more from personal experience than from that of others.

To be abrasive is to be evasive.

The meeker the weaker, the stronger the wronger.

Lies today spread like swarming flies.

New products solve old problems and birth new.

Deafening silence is loud disapproval.

To be a decent capably functioning member of society, and to remain a decent human being, is a trying challenge for the best of us.

To know is to understand, and to understand is to be kindly disposed, and to be kindly disposed is to embrace, not fight your fellow humans.

Goodness is often born of fear, but mayhem is fear's more common child.

Difference should stir curiosity, not animosity.

Fame is fickle fortune.

Our trials and tribulations make or break us.

Christ was the spark that lit the Christian-Judeo flame.

A timely recognition of personal limitations, and a conscientious cultivation of one's capabilities, is to come to grips and terms with self and life.

Decided points of view are prickly burs.

People think too highly of themselves, and are judged too severely by others.

Youth is lyric, age is tragic!

Those of few words are laconic or moronic.

The past is memory, the future is possibility, the present is an actuality.

To dispel the gloom of death, one need but accept one's mortality.

Self-preservation is life's sole passion.

Capitalism has its hounds, and they know no bounds.

Fences are poor defences.

Warfare is mankind's folly of follies.

Romantic love is but raw sexuality.

The mother-child bond is the most powerful and most enduring of human relationships.

A little foresight attenuates the shock of tomorrow's untoward surprises.

When all is known, nothing is chance.

Profit trumps privacy.

God's world is but a poor facsimile of man's world.

Fabricate a thought, when on the spot.

A driverless car is a headless driver.

An epigram a day keeps boredom away.

Imponderables tax the mind, and leave little behind.

Morality should not become a liability.

Death fertilizes life.

The real is actual, the ideal is but possible.

Romantic infatuation and alcoholic intoxication are common inebriations.

Why reality is what it is, is beyond both reason and imagination.

The female squats, the male squirts, and a new creature emerges.

Mankind's spiral evolution will end with mankind's viability.

Animals are lamed, when tamed.

The male is stronger, but the female lasts longer.

Vengeance, though sweet, is anything but meet.

All living things were not what they are, and are not what they will be.

All living matter is but a passing presence of the life force.

Reality is, was, and will be a constant becoming.

We come from nowhere, move in space, change in time, and nothing's chance.

Actuality and dream are but two sides of the same coin.

Life is not dream, it becomes dream.

Humans differ from each other but incidentally.

Nothing is right and nothing is wrong, for what is right is also wrong.

The man and woman relationship has always been more battlefield than playground.

Not to sow, is not to reap.

Everything has its consequences.

The promiscuous woman is a tramp, the promiscuous man is a rover.

Statistics are information and not solution.

When in, but not of, it's best to get out

Likes and dislikes are alarmingly capricious.

Mankind has always been more given to kneejerk opinion than to thoughtful informed argument.

Education is force-feeding of much, a digestion of little.

The more havoc men wreak, the sooner women will peak.

Let women go their way, and let men go theirs.

Life is a game that everyone plays and nobody wins.

The East was not the better for its opium and the West is not likely to be the better for its marijuana.

Disease cure is trumped by disease prevention.

War is a problem, not a cure.

Love is a pain and hate is a bane.

Driverless cars and headless drivers are of a kind.

Virtuality is a daydream, reality is a nightmare.

'Tis right or wrong, but alone in context.

Too many talk too much about too little.

Conversation reveals education.

The hurried are our harried.

Packaging sells it, money buys it.

Too many think too little about thinking.

Youth will have its way, but time will have its say.

The daring will not hesitate, and the hesitant will not dare.

Thinkers ruminate, and doers fabricate.

Be good to be good, and not just to avoid punishment.

Our laconic are of few words, and our taciturn are of none.

Complexity and confusion prepare the way for manipulation and exploitation.

Better to speak firmly than to shout loudly.

Choice, once a privilege, has become a chore.

Lies, like corruption, have become common coin.

Truth is admirable, lies are profitable.

The human being's conflicting natural and cultured selves have and will ever be at serious odds with each other.

To really know, is a challenge, to really understand, is a nightmare.

Unlike the language of mathematics, verbal language is verbose, clumsy and imprecise.

Digitalia's plethora of absurd apps and devices is trivializing, not enhancing life.

Robotization does much for industry, and nothing for culture.

Some people are different with a vengeance and with a purpose.

Science explains, religion proclaims.

Religion is a world of beliefs, science is a world of facts.

All is flux, nothing is final.

Heed need, curb want.

Youth is tomorrow, age is yesterday.

Youth holds promise, while age lies fallow.

Relativity is theory, not practice.

America is as little Democracy as Russia is Communism.

Males and females are as different from each other as are fathers and mothers.

Indispensables are as obligating as liberating.

Goodness is good of, and good for.

Don' t just bash and trash, assess and redress.

Pluralism and Democracy march to different drummers.

Multiculturism and Democracy are oil and water.

Train for physical skills, and educate for mental thrills.

Advertising has become skillful lying.

Education has lost its old lure, and training demands less effort and rewards more liberally.

Moderation is much praised but little practised.

A good day's work deserves a good day's pay.

The blind hear, and the deaf see.

The rich become richer, and the poor become poorer.

Moderation is honored in its breach and not in its practice.

Language is more convenience than it is precision.

We know too little, think too little, and act too rashly.

When all else fails, usage prevails.

Success depends no less upon ambition and tenacity than upon brains.

Instant gratification invites brief satisfaction.

Selection is choice, election is chance.

Trust takes wing, when corruption moves in.

Be mindful of purpose and aware of consequences.

Emerging cultures fret and labor, while dying cultures are given to revelry and play.

People change history, and history changes people.

Life is as futile as death is final.

Life is for the taking!
Some make the best of it,
And others make the worst of it.

Ours is a messy world, and likely to remain a messy world.

A mess it is!
Sex is a compulsive mess, and birth a joyful one.
Life itself is a hell of a mess, and death a very sad one.
All in all, all's a messy mess!

When popular embrace of technology's plethora of trivial devices and apps moved in, societal sanity moved out.

The Old World is on its deathbed, and the New is still powerless to be born.

A culture's beliefs and values are its compass and its ballast.

Bombast yes, bombs no.

Aloneness is an existential fact, not an affliction.

For most, life is an ordeal, not a Sunday picnic.

Life is never what it was, or will be.

Individualists opt for independence, the more community-minded prefer interdependence.

A balancing of mental and physical activity is salutary for both mind and body.

Archetypically, the few lead and the many follow.

Guns and humans are a lethal partnership.

Sex tears apart no less than it brings together.

Leave something—anything—to evidence your stay on earth.

Human beings are the deadliest of God's many wondrous creatures.

The quick react faster, but the fast get there quicker.

To insure, to ensure, and to assure, are birds of a different feather.

The early bird is hungrier than its tardy fellows.

Tend to business, and business will tend to you.

The talented are often troubled, while the troubled are rarely talented.

Niceties are diplomatic subtleties.

Love can be sexless, and sex can be loveless.

When excitement becomes habit, excitement becomes boredom.

Each is a hybrid: something of a man and something of a woman.

Legality and morality agree more than they differ.

The legal is more fluid than fixed, and the moral is more fixed than fluid.

Mankind's beliefs and truths are but pious hope and noble fiction.

The optimists make the best of it, the pessimists make the worst of it, and in both cases for all too little reason.

The active persist, the lethargic resist.

The uninformed know too much, the informed know too little.

Women tend to accommodate, men prefer to debate.

Respect even those who deserve no respect.

The driven are driven for many reasons, some laudable, others very questionable.

Conventional wisdom is a very provincial wisdom

The homely are no less distractive than the comely are attractive.

Some work because they know no better.

Mr. Notorious attracts attention, while Mr. Good gets no mention.

Communication with anyone, anywhere and at any time, is electronic capability, not communication.

Young, ambitious, talented entrepreneurs have fashioned an exciting electronic world for the young and the naïve.

Our yesterdays do not die when our todays dawn, and our todays live on in our tomorrows.

An exciting electronic "thing culture" has had its upstart day, it's time for a more intimate and more rewarding "human culture" to have its sway.

The swamp is life, the desert is death.

Change is the reality of life.

Too much cloys, and too little annoys.

Deference extends a hand, rebuff displays a fist.

To fawn is affection, to flatter is deception.

Too much explanation is more obfuscation than clarification.

The literal is bare and direct, the figurative is colorful and suggestive.

To poets, words are release and relief.

Loquacity invites opacity.

Most truths are but conventionalized opinions.

Agreement spells peace, disagreement invites war.

Slow readers absorb as much as they can, while fast readers only take away what they want.

Multi-tasking takes its toll.

Worst enemies can become best friends.

The deepest of friendships are usually of a gender.

Competitors can be friends, but often become foes.

Brain is organ, mind is function.

A life without direction, is blind and shallow existence.

Men are taken with sex, women are more given to love.

Procrastination is brief relief, and trailing bad conscience.

Men break out in anger, women break down in tears.

Life is struggle and grief, death is release and relief.

To be idle can be unfortunate, to be lazy is reprehensible.

Say your say, then call it a day.

Impatience is abrasive, patience is balm.

See a brother in the other.

Water seeks its lowest level.

Absolute truth is at best but strongly held opinion.

All is relative, nothing is absolute.

The thin smile or grin, the fat moan or groan.

What might ensue, if Buddha, Mohammed and Christ were, per chance, to meet in some solemn retreat.

Butter for the top few, and skim milk for the bottom many.

Learn to think, before you try to think.

To learn ever more, one need but explore.

America's world of sports: too much ado about too little.

The whole is only as strong as the part.

Think a new thought, do a good deed, and smile all the while.

Too much cloys, too little roils.

Treasure the indispensable, and discard the dispensable.

To assist physically, is to be rewarded psychologically.

Children are the doing of their parents.

Parents fashion and are fashioned by their children.

General discontentment is a contagious malady.

Morality not exercised is morality excised.

Ours is a world of opinions that range from the ridiculous to the sublime. The former deserve but short shrift, and the latter should be digested.

Don't clean what is not dirty.

Morality, once very obliging, has today become quite accommodating.

Bloviate or masticate, don't double date.

Animosity knows no generosity.

Memories are life relived.

To trust is good, to verify is better.

To become your person is good for you, to become your job is good for your employer.

Don't expect respect, if you yourself don't respect.

The timid are too cautious, and the reckless are too careless.

We are damned if we do, and we are damned if we don't.

Women opt for togetherness, while men prefer aloneness.

What better than mental-physical wellbeing?

Men have their muscles and women have their wiles.

The human male is as destructive as he is creative.

Fear and anger spread fear and anger.

To be sorry alone, does not atone.

Most diets are nothing more than pious hope.

To eat regardless of consequences, has its consequences.

Expectations have their frustrations.

To expect is to burden.

We are more taken with things than given to humans.

Too much attention is being given to things technological, and too little to things human: a cultural imbalance, that does not augur well for the Western World.

The much we know about reality, is but a smidgen of the vast unknown.

Given its bloody past, mankind will very likely eventually self-destruct.

That man was created after the image of God, is a figment of human conceit.

Human folly is feasting on technology's frivolity.

In cultural decline, essentials become incidentals, and incidentals become essentials.

Women are intuitively responsive, while men tend to be actionally reflexive.

Children play, carefree, adults work and worry.

Female had hearth and children, the male provided and protected. Such once it was but is no more.

Hate fuels fight, love invites intimacy.

Demeanor and dress the world address.

Ours is a blind trek from nowhere to nowhere.

That humans are not what they could and should be is obvious, and that this is unlikely ever to change for the better, is no less obvious.

Too many are insatiable, and too many are unquenchable.

The arrogant are ever right and never wrong.

The experts know they know, and the unschooled think they know.

We come and we go.
Whence and whither,
We'll never know.

Cultural dumbing-down, in general, and the cultural dumbing-down of political discourse, in particular, do not augur well for the Western World, in general, and for the U.S.A. in particular.

Capitalism is a power, populism but a voice.

Ugliness, like beauty, is both concept and judgment.

Epigrams are witty mental pastime.

Quality is opinion, quantity is fact.

When everyone has a voice, no one is heard.

To raise one's voice, is to be heard, but not heeded.

To be heeded, is to be both heard and appreciated.

Until one has something to say, silence should hold sway.

Treasure your measure of wellbeing.

Each thinks, feels and does what he/she is.

Concrete words have their precise *conventional meaning*, while abstract words have their *ranging shades of individual meaning.*

Curiosity kills rats not cats.

Trust only, when trust is merited.

Peace is Heaven, wars are Hell.

Every action has its reaction.

Feelings are primary, spontaneous and compelling, while thought is secondary, calculated and imploring.

For all too many males, fathering begins and ends with bedroom frolicking.

Christianity's heavenly hierarchy is but a spare replica of our earthly hierarchies.

For the male in rut, every woman's a slut.

Education is more informative than it is transformative.

Self-knowledge and self-realization are possibility, not probability.

Feelings are reflexive, thought is reflective.

One is never what one was, and will never be what one is.

The nobility was courtly and portly, the peasants were uncouth and lean.

Creativity is free ranging intelligence.

It is easier to say than to do.

The top orders, the bottom obeys.

Things, of themselves, are not right or wrong, we only think so.

Violent language peaks in violent action.

Expletives relieve and aggrieve.

Memory is life's ballast.

Much of literature is less fiction than it is transfigured autobiography.

Literary criticism is all too often more fiction than the fiction criticized.

Failed authors often become successful scholars and publishers.

Half-hearted interest guarantees half-hearted success.

The what, whence, whither and why of life, are purely academic.

Seeds and plants alternate in an endless dance of life.

The Life Force is a timeless continuum of endless births and deaths.

Of itself, nothing is good or bad, thin or fat, beautiful or ugly, sacred or profane, but in a relationship.

Do the best you can, then rest content upon your laurels.

The powerful are wealthy, and the wealthy are powerful.

Too many two-legged creatures never were human, or lost their humanity.

To know oneself well, is to know the other better.

Wealth is not always good, and poverty is not always bad.

What is self-wrought need not be bought.

Don't spend what you don't have.

"To have nothing, is to be nothing." So some would say.

Evolution is but life adapting to changing circumstances.

The manifestations of life that do not adapt to reality's changing circumstances, fall by life's waysides.

Emotions drive, reason guides.

Heaven and hell are an earthly presence, not a future possibility.

We're not born good or bad, but we become either or both.

Rock your own boat, don't rock mine.

Feed your angels, and starve your demons.

The new is commonly indebted to the old.

Freedom unequal, is freedom abused.

Sophisticated electronic communication has both improved and worsened human relationships.

Like the weather, climate is ever changing.

Men would have their own world, as do women, and children too.
Each world differs from the others.
And each is the richer for these differences.

Wars are deadly, sports are only rough, but each is of the other's stuff.

It is high time for racial and gender harassment to pack their bags and leave

For the taciturn introvert, more given to serious thought than to frivolous play, life is a somber arena, not a boisterous playground.

Convenience is a seduction not a challenge.

Corporations are the empires of the financial world.

Difference stirs animosity no less than curiosity.

Problems seek their solutions.

An honest question deserves an honest answer.

Too much fun, is no fun.

The easy sedates, the hard irritates.

Brawn at dawn, brains at twilight.

Most people do what they have to do, not what they like to do, and they're also the better for it.

The familiar comforts, the unfamiliar discomforts.

Every religion dies with its last believers.

But for mankind's trials and tribulations, hopes and fears, desperation and resourceful imagination, there would be no gods and no beyond.

What fantastic an array of beliefs and gods it is, that trails mankind's spiritual evolution.

What each is, is what he/she chose to be, wittingly or unwittingly.

Schooling should not be education or training, but a meld of the two possibilities.

Mankind's world of today is as good and as bad as it has ever been and ever will be.

Do something, be something!
Don't just waste away
In trivial play.

Multiculturalism has its multiproblems.

Not to change when change is in order, is to remain the poorer for it.

Not all gifts are free.

To eat to your heart's content, may end to fat body's discontent.

To know, is to know better.

The introvert is self-preoccupied, the extrovert is self-satisfied.

The expert is a severe judge, the layman a lenient one.

The sickly are likely to frown, while the healthy tend to clown.

In army parlance, defeat has become strategic retreat.

Mutual accommodation invites mutual appreciation.

When all is said and done, it is only at birth and at death, that the lofty and lowly are one.

To think and to do, and to do and to think, will leave you in the pink.

Self-discontent is no less common than other-envy.

Small misdeeds, like tiny seeds, can spread like weeds.

Mental and physical activity guarantees longevity.

Not to defer when deference is in order, is to be out of order.

The wealthy make money, the poor make a living.

Simplicity makes for clarity, while complexity ends in obscurity.

Managers once knew more and managed less, today's managers know less and manage more.

Goods once commonly fetched, are today commonly delivered.

The ailing bleat, the hardy shout.

We are paradoxically over-informed, and left under-informed.

Each begins a something, and can become a someone.

Life's complexities are life's nemeses.

Wishes are desperate hopes.

Change what you can, and accept what you must.

What is good or bad for me is not so for everyone.

Pure genders there are none.

To accept the inevitable, is to make death palatable.

Man is both drone and working bee.

Men are here, to service the source of life.

Sloth is no less exhausting than work.

Exhilarating work is exciting play.

Buy what you want to buy, and not what the seller wants to sell.

When all becomes but gasp and sigh, it may be time to say goodbye.

There's still life, when there's still pain and strife.

Would that life were, what we would have it be.

We kill at will, and never have our fill.

Dying is life's final act.

Digitalia is a success-drunk gadgetry world.

To have more on the one hand, is to have less on the other.

Politicians are more given to empty proclamations than to meaningful transformations.

Wise fools know, what wise men don't.

Religions have always accounted for the unaccountable.
And the lame will walk,
When the heavens open,
And earth closes shop.

Life is an unholy mess—more or less!

To be more mindful of death, is to be more appreciative of life.

Surfeit cloys! Digitalia's gadgetry madness has had its heyday.

All too common contrite apologies and ardent promises, are all too commonly more impression than correction

Freedom accords and freedom exacts.

Slavery has little redeeming grace.

All that *is,* eventually becomes a *was.*

Circumstances birth both the haughty and the humble.

Everything has its price.

Humans don't know, they only think, that animals don't think.

Different intelligences is a poor substitute for *different skills.*

The virtual world is rapidly encroaching upon the actual.

Our earth's changing climate is nothing new; only the extent and rate of this ever-changing is something new.

One man's treasure can be another man's trivia.

The alone are not necessarily the lonely, and the lonely are not necessarily alone.

Humility has become history.

To work at home, and to shop online,
Is to better husband your time.

Mankind romanticized sex, and unwittingly sowed the seeds of expectation and disillusionment.

Guess is aided by imagination, opinion is influenced by information, and judgment is buttressed by reason.

Too much that is said, is but a motley spread.

Sport once meant for only you and me,
Is today a massive industry.
Colossal stadiums have shadowed lowly playgrounds,
Throngs are thrilled, and players and owners enriched!
But is the world the better for this change?

Do unto others, as you would have them do unto you.
A wise guideline!
Do unto others, as others do unto you.
A questionable prompt!

Order succeeds anarchy, and anarchy succeeds order, and ne'er this succession will end.

The battle of the sexes has ever changed, but will never cease.

Racism will continue as long as there are races.

Self-knowledge and self-realization are approximation not realizations.

To learn to do anything is half the battle of doing something.

The puffed up are but display and play.

A leader, not a follower be.

Loud mouths will be heard, but should not be heeded.

Better to lead than to push.

The poor are wealthy in some regards, and the wealthy are poor in many regards.

No one is no one, everyone is someone.

Religions make the best of it, corporations make a mess of it.

Think a thought then ponder it, and you will be the better for it.

Loaf if you will, but work if paid.

The wealthy reckon, that they need but beckon to have their way.

Life becomes sufferable, when suffering becomes tolerable.

Some people become, and more people just happen.

'Tis not chance or choice, but inevitability.

One's person and circumstances account for one's feelings, thoughts and actions.

Too many people live without living, leaving no imprint to recall them.

When the willing can't and the unwilling won't, the shit hits the fan.

Libertarians are unabashed apostles of liberty, given to history, philosophy and psychology.

Some prevail in spite of, and others prevail because of.

What's in it for me, has become a common query.

MeTooism of whatever kind, is ever in danger of becoming a questionable grind.

One person's profundity, is another person's banality.

Brilliant ideas are rare gems mined by the rare mind.

Arch conservatives are constipated, and arch liberals are diarrhetic.

We do what we are, and we are what we do.

Some live to write—a calling.
Some write to live—a living.

Violence is a reaction, not a remedy.

Like alcohol, love is a commodity that intoxicates and often ends in a hangover.

The bigger the better, is America's mantra of mantras.

The shakers and makers, are society's thinking-doers.

How better to honor the dead than by remembering them?

Some are too busy living to give death more than a passing thought.

Join the throng, you can't go wrong! One persuasion.
Sit and think, you can't go wrong! Another persuasion.

Populism brushes expertise aside, and embraces ignorance.

Not to be mindful of and helpful to the needy, is to be something less than human.

MeTooism's likely to remain more vindictive than corrective.

Activity is commotion, action is promotion.

For too many men, women are here but for the taking.

To command language, is to command respect.

It is important to know when to talk, and when not to talk.

To become healthier, wealthier and wiser, curb your appetite and moderate your menus.

The well-being of the business world trumps that of the people at large.

Sexual intercourse exemplifies male assertiveness, agressiveness, and female reticence and accommodation.

To have no goal is to have no path.

Religion is the balm of balms.

Some people change their minds as often as the chameleon changes its colors.

To blame has become a political game.

To read many novels is to live many lives.

Life gives and takes, humans take and give.

Heed your need and weed your want.

Pomposity is an atrocity.

What challenges, advances.

The soft touch can be as effective as the iron fist.

Some are self-driven, others have to be driven.

Our todays are born of our yesterdays.

Treasure your yesterdays; but for them, there would be no todays.

Belief comforts, disbelief troubles!

Like flowers, cultures germinate, grow and flower, then wither and die.

Rules and regulations are guidelines to be heeded, not annoying restrictions to be flouted.

Your bed is of *your* making.

Try until you die.

To be nice, can be a vice.

Humans don't die, they are left to feast or to fry.

Rats do chase cats, but only figuratively so.

Where but in Erewhon, do rats chase cats.

Our many would-be-noteworthies, are just that and nothing more.

For the military mind, life is war, victory and defeat.
For the lay thinker, life is struggle, success and failure.

It is life that goes, and not death that comes.

Life takes wing on the flow of one's last breath.

Grasp what your arm can reach, and not what your mind would have.

Ought to is more plea than command, and *must* is more command than plea.

A new thought every day, will keep mental rust away.

Humans are to their photos what paper books are to electronic books.

When yesterdays become more present than todays, it's probably high time to pack and leave.

The sound of body and mind, are few and hard to find.

Much that is today, is as it was yesterday and as it will tomorrow be.

Not to know Earth for what it is, is not to appreciate Heaven for what it is.

Mankind's fragile civilizations have ever come and gone. The natural world, in contrast, endures as it goes its evolving way.

To hear is chance, to listen is intent.

People who really never live, never really die.

Thinkers are little taken with action, and doers are little given to reflection.

For many today, Life Before High Tech has already become nostalgic-tinged memory.

The present leaves us a past, and gives us a future.

The inept fumble and the clumsy tumble.

The female knows pain, and the male inflicts pain.

Essential human appetites can be dulled or sublimated, but not eradicated.

Revenge is passion, reconciliation is reflection. Little and quality trumps much and mediocrity.

Someday, mankind's rather primitive binary view of reality and life, will give way to a more nuanced view of both.

Pollution is a problem and not a solution.

Less civility means more hostility.

To be bad, is just as human as to be good.

The willful are hopeful.

Anger, hatred, violence, are a vicious sequence.

Religion is mankind's placebo of placebos.

When traditional men bark, traditional women hark.

To be without a conscience, is to be without a compass.

Sex is akin to a military spin.

The thrill is in the hunt, not in the kill.

Humans are of, and live in, both a spiritual and material world.

Indolence is a state of mind, laziness is a state of body.

Quantity is a poor substitute for quality.

Cats are self-minded, and dogs are master-minded.

To be bored is to be boring.

The hale and hearty primp and party.

The male, once protector and provider, has become a companion and an associate.

To be knowledgeable and reflective, is to be effective.

Good learners become good teachers.

Not to remember is not to know, and not to know is not to be in the flow.

Thoughtful observation is an education.

The blame game is a lame game.

To forget, is to regret.

The apathetic are pathetic.

Genes alone don't ever have their way,
Life-style too, and circumstances have their say.

Moralists admonish ad nauseam.

Death of life a futile struggle makes.

Few in life do but observe, more participate, and most do both.

To be mindful of propriety, is to be appreciated by society.

One can't exchange oneself, but one can change oneself.

If you have you are, and if you do not have, you are not.

To be busy is good, but to be diligent is better.

To know better is good, to be better is better.

Things are never as good or as bad as they first seem to be.

Life is what it is, and not what we would like it to be.

Life on earth is a reality, heaven and hell are figment of the imagination.

Aim high and settle for less.

Birth *and* death are part of life.

Expect more of yourself, and do something about it.

Marijuana promises to become a popular panacea.

Though sweet, revenge is not meet.

Self-realization is aspiration, not attainable possibility.

Populism knows little and cares less.

Doubt is good cause for pause and reflection.

Life is a losing battle.

Drugs are a Godsend and a devilish delight.

Populism's world of uninformed opinion has replaced the informed opinion of the world of expertise.

Man does not live by bread alone—a slice of salami helps.

Life is a deadly game.

The transformation of inert matter to conscious organic matter, is beyond explanation.

To pay one's debts is good, but not to make debts is better.

Better to emulate than to envy.

The wise are inconspicuous, the foolish are ubiquitous.

Tend to the living and remember the dead.

Fear and pain can be gain.

Politically, nothing seems to mean what it seems to say.

One is but rarely fully right or fully wrong.

To have aught, is to be someone,
To have nought, is to be no one.

That each living thing is *generally* of a kind and *specifically* unique, is a miraculous phenomenon.

There is little on earth, that mankind would not have be otherwise.

Life's imponderables will never cease their teasing of human thought.

Cultures come and cultures go, always have, and always will.

Change with change, or fall aside.

Ride with the tide, or be sucked under.

Tomorrow will be something new, and something of today and yesterday.

Tomorrow will see more robots and more fat people.

America and Russia have had their day.
China and India will soon hold sway.

Emotional thinkers are poetic, rational thinkers are prosaic.

Decency is primary, beauty, brains and brawn are secondary.

Some do good who are good, and some do good to become good.

Some day, humans will be good, just to be good, and not in response to reward or punishment.

Dilettantes are sensitive and talented dabblers in the arts,
More aesthetes than artists,
More self-indulgent than committed,
And more personality than person!

Lies are for many but alternatives to truths.

Addictions are afflictions that know no restriction.

Fanatics are but self-anointed true believers.

Authority is legalized power.

To chafe less and appreciate more can be a very rewarding chore.

To have nothing, is oft better than to have something.

Exceptionals go their own way and do their own thing.

People are only as effective as they are persuasive.

An epigram says something unusual, unusually.

Actuality disappoints, possibility inspires.

Women seek security, men seek victory.

Life's battle is done, when yesterdays, todays and tomorrows become one.

The willing are often not able, and the able are often not willing.

That matriarchies will soon supplant patriarchies, is no longer one of life's uncertainties.

When, what once was right becomes wrong, and what was once wrong becomes right, one culture has gone, and another has come.

Life has its way, and each goes his/her own way.

Two and two was once four, but that now, is no more.

Mankind's in a rush, little's what it was.

Not to rush, is less to err.

The Electronics Age is more exciting rush than cultural blush.

Respect when merited, *and* when less than due.

When bonds are frail, all is likely to fail,
When bonds are strong, nothing seems to go wrong.

If made stronger, it'll last longer.

Men confer, women defer, and children prefer.

Skills, not luck, will pay your bills.

All is not for nought, though all becomes but nought.

Our Judeo-Christian culture is dead and a technologized business world has birthed.

Thoughts inspire, feelings activate, and actions satisfy.

To be different, is to be received differently.

What becomes one, need not become another.

To be different, makes a difference.

Some are quick and some are slow, and why that's so, is hard to know.

When the old step down, the young step up, and all is what it was.

Profound and creative minds are few in number,
Nimble minds are more numerous,
Wanting minds are plentiful,
And lazy minds are bountiful.

A win for women need not be a loss for men.

Compromise not hard won, is not wise.

The best of transactions are those that benefit both parties.

The mantra "ever faster, ever more, ever better," invites ever more breakdowns.

Marijuana is likely to be what is has been: more indulgence than panacea.

Contentment is more based on what one has than upon how much one has.

What is gathered in life, is scattered by death.

Home is an idea not a house.

To improve the approach, is to improve the result.

To do nothing can often achieve something.

To compel stirs opposition, to persuade invites cooperation.

Oh to be older when young, and oh to be younger when old!

The hurried are the harried, and the harried are the scatter-brained.

Life only appears to have free rides.

Absolutes are absolute folly.

In form, epigrams are fettered, in substance, they are free.

Life has a spot and role for everyone.

Life's unpredictable interplay of chance and choice, can make or break.

Give generously and take sparingly.

Sustenance is life's primary drive. All else is secondary.

Today's truths are tomorrow's fictions.

Human beings are arch dreamers and schemers.

Mankind's world has always been a glorious mess, sometimes better, sometimes worse.

Emotions know no reason.

Ignorance is not a badge of honor.

Knowledge is fruitful, ignorance is sterile.

Each is but a passing presence.

We do because we can, and we can because we do.

Sweet duets do all too oft become but bitter duels.

To ponder whence, why, whither, can leave you in a dither.

The powerful everywhere have ever done
What the robber giant Procrustes did:
Stranger guests were greeted with a bed
And all were stretched to fit that iron stead!

To strive and to struggle, though all is in vain
Is our dour lot and our endless pain.

Money corrupts both rich and poor, and both young and old.

Treat the other decently, not gingerly or roughly.

Marijuana is mankind's latest elixir.

Hatred and threat, inhumanity abet.

Civility should be mothered, not orphaned.

Too many entertainers become but popular freaks.

The line between pseudo art and real art, has become very fine.

The unusually different alone, does art not make.

The art world has always incorporated a touch of freakish otherness.

Some humor is not humorous, and some questions have no answer.

Life is something far more, and something far different from but one person's view of it.

That "passion burns to its own destruction," does surely not diminish it.

Life burdens, death unburdens.

To discuss is to resolve, to argue is to contend.

In the word's original meaning, everyone who is someone, is something of a freak.

To peak short of one's goal, is more common lot than not.

When all is said, and all is done, life's much grief and little fun.

Nothing is here to stay.
Mankind's days are numbered.
The end is but a question
Of when and how!

That mankind's aspirations and endeavours
May ultimately be but vain and futile,
Is a dour conviction that plagued Old Greece
And found its expression in Sisyphus, hill and stone.

People are too commonly permissive of the self and dismissive of others.

Love returns love, and hate returns hate.

To only see what is displeasing, is to become oneself unpleasant.

The content respond with a smile, the angry with a glare.

To punish oneself, can be to reward oneself.

To deprive oneself, is to punish or reward oneself.

Punishment can be twice rewarding.

Mens sana in corpore sano! Life's greatest gifts.

Reciprocity can be atrocity.

Too many are conditioned, not educated.

Dance enhances romance.

Unspoken expectations have their untoward consequences.

Silent expectations are abominations.

To mean well is good, to do good is better.

Gird your loins: Life's getting worse not better.

Humans assess, cats stalk.

The admonitions of our culture's thinking few, have been muffled by populism's vacuous din.

Greed heeds no admonishments, and knows no limits.

Too few pause to reason why.

To learn to think, is to rise from the brink.

Relent, repent, and then try anew with a new view.

Honesty is demanding, but also morally rewarding.

Work should be both satisfying and rewarding.

Play recuperates, work maintains.

Freedom can be as debilitating as it can be exhilarating.

Mankind knows, but little heeds.

Compromises are provisional agreements, not solutions.

Guilt is trial and punishment.

One culture's justice is not every country's justice.

Justice is more possibility than actuality.

The voice of the untutored man, should be heard, but only judiciously heeded.

Multicultural democracy is a pipe dream.

Life has needs and wants, death has neither.

Dispose of the old, before beginning anew.

Pettiness and insecurity find their compensation.

The physically-wanting, oft find a niche in the mental world.

Empty-minded populism has made a low-brow religion of professional sport.

A global digital culture has begun to crystalize around a worldwide religion, called Business.

For society to function ably, tentative truths—and all truths are tentative—must be tentatively treated as absolute truths.

Women are guardians, men are marauders.

Mankind destructs as rapidly as it constructs.

The richer the rich, the poorer the country.

Disinformation only serves its disseminators.

A closed mind is a sick mind.

An open mind is a crafty mind.

Persistent effort paves the way.

The unctuous ingratiate, the rambunctious grate.

To interest oneself in the interests of another, is to find an appreciative brother.

America's "manifest destiny" and "messianic mission" are grotesquery at its best.

Hope brightens one's way, and lightens one's burdens.

Time will tell, but only if one has ears.

CEO's play musical chairs.

To save is a passion for some, to spend, a passion for others.

If a person is to change for the better, ingrained mental and physical habits have to be changed.

Money makes and breaks.

A smile invites a smile, a frown puts down.

Day is for work and play, night is best for rest.

But for memory, nothing would be what it is.

Ere long, Christianity's heavenly host will find its station in history's pantheon of spent deities.

For many, to elevate the different other, is to lower the self.

To give without expectations, is to remain of good will.

To upbraid is to downgrade.

When much becomes little, it's time to resettle.

Wall street is glow and glee today, and doom and gloom tomorrow.

Immigrants are criminals today, and good citizens tomorrow.
It all depends upon political winds!

America's proverbial "open arms" have become closed fists.

The like embrace, the unlike confront.

America welcomes or rejects quite indiscriminately.

Where there is no civility, there is no community.

Familiarity both binds and blinds.

To tend to today, is to be prepared for tomorrow.

Faces are more telling than words.

Women are becoming more masculine, and men are becoming more feminine.

Good memories are precious treasure troves.

But for memory, all would slip away, all too quickly.

The *human condition* does not warm the cockles of many hearts.

Life is a mess because humans are a mess, and god has left the scene.

Mankind changes at the edges, but not at the core.

Wealth and power are fickle and flighty.

Corruption is a very rewarding seduction.

For younger generations, the tidal rush of digital novelty has been exhilarating.
For the old, the tidal loss of the familiar, has been appalling.

In the world of today's spreading populism,
The untutored know better,
Unqualified nonentities assume authority,
And mediocrity has become the norm.

Our ingenious Electronics Age, together with our resourceful Corporate World,
May signal the pending demise of our fading Judeo-Christian culture.
Or are Electronics Age and Corporate World
Forerunners of a vibrant new World Culture?

Beginnings have ends,
Ends had beginnings.

A cultural mess may be a last chapter, or a first chapter.

Earth is for the many, and heaven is for the few.

Religions do not explain, they elaborate and obfuscate.

A smirk is not likely to elicit a smile.

Suicide is attraction not solution.

To write an epigram each day, will help to keep boredom at bay.

It's not race, not gender nor age, but one's person that makes a difference, and leaves an imprint.

All humans are immigrants, literally and figuratively. Something to remember.

We come with nothing, and leave with nothing, from nowhere to nowhere, a nightmare.

We are all alike, but critically different.

The different have always both attracted and repelled.

Modern Western culture has become progressively more materialistic and practical, and its centers of learning have become progressively more training than educational institutions.

In tomorrow's world, the male-female sexual bond, is likely to continue, though slightly changed, while the general male-female interaction, is likely to experience a drastic change.

Most change is little change, and little for the better.

A virulent disease is sweeping across the landscape. Radical automation has flown the coop!

Educate where you can, and train where you must.

Automation has its plus and its minus: It can both liberate and devastate.

Rape is a violent criminal action that demands severe punishment. General harassment is unacceptable behavior that deserves reprimand.

Paradoxically, anti-Semitism has helped to keep the Jewish community intact.

In its wild and futile efforts to grapple with its plethora of socio-political problems, America might do well to look to Canada's mode of operation.

When threatened, the wagons circle.

The novel attracts, and the convenient is prized.

What sells well is raucously acclaimed, and what sells poorly is quietly shelved.

The lame don't sprint, nor do crows warble.

Immigrants are humans in need, not foreigners on the prowl.

To care for one another, is to be cared for.

To sleep at night, is to be prepared for the day.

We are but visitors, and soon go our way.

Automation can humans decommission.

Physical impairment triggers mental compensation.

Noise deafens the ears and dulls the mind.

Neologisms are new verbal sprouts.

Procreation is a drive, sex is an appetite.

Social media has become a mania.

Busy heads and busy mind, little time for mischief find.

Don't try to fly, should you have no wings.

In prayer, the hopeless may find hope.

The poor are the needy, the wealthy are the greedy.

Choose, don't just deign to help the needy.

Better to communicate than to condescend.

To interact, yes. To intertangle, no!

Reality is an endless repetition of repetitions.

Everyone comes and goes, but whence and whither, nobody knows.

Humans are but a functioning mass of flesh, blood and bones,
encased in a protective skin.

Bitter experience taught the Greeks of old,
That impossible venture was folly and futile.
Icarus of the wax-bound wings and plunge,
Warned mankind for ages, but to no avail.

Convenient things and novelty,
Have become our age's addiction.
The human being, once focal concern,
Has almost become a thing of the past.

Sin is punished above,
Crime is punished below.
Humans are kept in tow,
Wherever they may go.

Races are different, countries no less,
Cultures are different, so too politics.
Religions are different, truths no less,
No wonders, indeed, that peace is so rare!

To ban war is a pipe dream,
To limit war to skirmishes, holds some appeal.

Remonstrations tend to the past, aspirations look to the future.

Habitual recollection and reflection make for a healthy mental diet.

Tomorrow's mental and physical health depends upon today's habits.

To make the best of one's self, is to sleep soundly.

Your health is your true wealth.

"Mens sana in corpore sano," will never cease to be life's gift of gifts.

To be kind and forgiving, is a major social lubricant.

Necessity awakens ingenuity.

The more informed and more reflective tend to be less active than judgmental.

Prisons harden or break, they do not remake.

Mankind is on a merry-go-round, that never closes its whirling rounds.

Little is wrought, when there's too much activity and too little thought.

Rehabilitate when possible, incarcerate when necessary.

The past recalls the present, and the present augurs the future.

Whence, wither and why, are the most gnawing of our many imponderables.

Most humans live, too many just exist.

Time does go its fleeting way, unconcerned and without delay.

The frivolous are playful, the serious are thoughtful.

Highly perceptive specialists are often blind generalists.

To cling to the evanescent, is to be left empty-handed.

Raw meals are probably as healthy as cooked meals. The difference is in the taste.

Too much change, is but for change, and not progress.

Decency is yours for the choosing.

Women deplore and implore, men explore and exploit,

Science argues *new* truths, and confirms *old*.

Work when you can, and rest when you must.

Much in life is inevitable, far less is choice.

Assumptions invite discord.

Equality is ideality, not possibility.

Each is a unique product of genes and circumstances.

In death, we fall into an unknown void, or rise to some blissful haven.

For good fortune and happiness,
We need not go afield.
What can be found afar,
Is ours to grasp wherever we are.

Take what you will, but please don't steal.

Credit cards loosen the purse, actual money tightens it.

Life is what it is, and what is made of it.

The hungry squirm, the sated burp.

Our socio-political world's in shambles,
Religion is spent, philosophy rent.
Technology and its corporations,
Have become our Golden Calves.

Wise it is, to think or do, before you pooh-pooh.

Not able to do aught, will leave you fraught.

Every living thing has its day, and then goes its way.

What is work for many, is play for some.

Need is affliction, greed is addiction.

The more you do, the more will be asked of you.

Humans without a moral compass, are ships without a helm or rudder.

Wanderers are more seekers than finders.

Thoughtful opinion deserves thoughtful response.

General mayhem marks the twilight of an old culture and the dawn of a new.

Generational friction has increased with the decline of generational commonality.

Commonality attracts, uniqueness distracts.

Good marketing will sustain, poor marketing is a bane.

Cash is for the tightwad, plastic is for the spendthrift.

Inflation means less for more.

That robots are performing ever more and ever better, will have challenging consequences for tomorrow's world.

Language was once a measure of a person's social standing.

Public school teachers have never enjoyed the prestige or the financial rewards they merit.

Professional sport has become a hard-nosed money-making industry.

Mammoth international corporations have become our modern political empires.

Revolutions are more raw power struggles, than commitment to socio-political improvement.

In our present socio-political disarray, everything seems to be going astray.

Civility in international politics and diplomacy, has become a thing of the past.

In the present growing international socio-political turmoil, nationalism has begun to assert itself anew.

Such as the papacy and the world's remaining monarchs, have become quaint oddities.

To focus on a human robot, is to lose sight of the human being.

Automate only when automation is more beneficial than damaging.

Each oak tree is what its acorn promises, and what circumstances hold in store.

The more we think, the more we think we know.

God created humans after his own image,
Humans are creating robots after their own image,
Robots will refashion their makers,
And where will it all end.

Moderation is both touted and flouted.

The diligent are energetic, the indolent are lethargic.

Love is a coat of many colors.

The acquisitive acquire, the inquisitive inquire.

To be alive, is to be on the prowl.

Sagacity is a result, not a reward.

Good health is but sound body and sound mind.

The living are driven to stay alive and to procreate.

From birth to death, humans become progressively more burdened.

Hopes of youth give way to the regrets of age.

Corruption is a temptation, to which political and financial
presences succumb all to readily and all too often.

For some free spirits, foul weather is not fit for work and fair
weather is too good for work.

Political jargon serves a purpose other than communication.

Women smile obligingly, men grin fleetingly.

In due time all will end, only to begin anew.

Hope alone will fall short of salutary change.

Hypersensitivity demands extreme caution.

The thick-skinned and the thin-skinned, do well to go their separate ways.

Some are natural bosses, more are would-be bosses.

Ultimately men will fail, and women will prevail.

Warfare is a passion, that will likely never go out of fashion.

To politically defame, is an old malicious game.

Too many are too intent upon self-elevation and other-depreciation.

Relative truths change, absolute truths transform.

We are what we allow life to make of us.

To be fully in, and of, the human scene, and yet to be thoughtfully detached, may for few, peak in wisdom.

Too many, rightfully or wrongfully, deem themselves to be leaders.

Greatness and grandeur appeal to many, who are made of but common stuff.

Wellbeing generates energy, and energy makes for wellbeing.

Just to dream of better possibility, changes nothing.

It does not take wealth and station to be a decent human being.

There are those who can do with little, and those who can't do with much.

The lowly, the humble, weak and meek, have little and inherit less.

Life gathers and accumulates, death just buries.

Life, if nothing else, asserts itself.

To know one's fellow human being, is to empathize.

Today's populism, born of our world's dying cultures,
Knows no truths, and has sidelined knowledge,
Extols kneejerk opinion, and toys freely with news,
Believes or disbelieves indiscriminately,
And has opted for low-brow subjectivity and relativism.

Einstein's lofty theory of relativity, has become our world's low-brow relativism.

To know is not enough, to do has to follow.

When inflation goes up, standard of living goes down.

Apology is not a remedy, it but assuages.

Anger is a commodity that is never in short supply.

Anger both relieves and peeves.

Certificates promise training, degrees promise education.

Time is born of whatever change.

Armageddon is the stuff of the imagination.

To be a racist in thought is immorality, to be a racist in word or deed, is criminality.

Not to change when change is in order, is to cut off one's nose to spite one's face.

What is heaven for some, is hell for others.

Absolute freedom of the individual would be the death of mankind.

Most individuals cherish only certain liberties, not absolute freedom.

Country folk holiday in cities, city dwellers opt for the open spaces.

Too much of anything, becomes a deadly drag.

Only some wild animals are the better for their domestication.

The old cling to what was, the young embrace the new.

To trust yourself, you must know yourself.

To be enterprising, imaginative, tenacious and persistent, is as rewarding as it is demanding.

Threats may intimidate, or infuriate, they never ingratiate.

The ordinary are our many, the gifted are our few.

Disturbing lies have become innocuous euphemistic alternative truths.

Things are making progressively more things than are human beings.

Daily newspaper accounts of sexual harassment, have for the peculiarly inquisitive, become something of a popular soap opera.

Nature and mankind go their separate ways.

Life is a steady flow and ebb of grief and joy.

Winter's ebb becomes spring's flow.

Our present world of countries, is likely in due time, to become a world of international corporations.

The World of Corporations has co-opted the World of Politics.

The business world's credo:
To grow, is to flourish,
To stagnate, is to perish.

Not to deceive, is of itself, no protection against deception.

Money elects politicians, and money legislates.

Democracy did not fly the coop, it was sent on its way.

Tomorrow is likely to see much more of today, before a new dawn breaks.

The familiar is habit, the novel is adventure.

To answer questions is to tell lies.

All that culturally was, is tattered and torn, and the new has yet to be born.

Mentally-lazy lane, has become a veritable bane.

Today's facts are tomorrow's fictions.

Take in want, and give when you can.

The left shoe is not fit for the right foot.

Require before you acquire.

The natural world, is God's dominion, the world of civilizations, is mankind's domain.

Take in need, and give in care.

Changes in person and circumstances, necessitate accordant changes in personal relationships.

Silent expectations invite smoldering disappointment.

To be of a community, curtails some of the individual's freedoms, but also adds others.

Biters bite, and are bitten.

The gypsies are everywhere, but nowhere at home.

The Jews have their own ballpark, and are equally at home and capable, in the ballpark of the world.

When distressed, perception becomes deception.

Promises unfulfilled, are seeds of ill will.

Let be the alone, who are not lonely.

The sad who are mourning, are no less normal than the joyous, who are rejoicing.

Life is an endless sowing and harvesting.

To be fat, is to bear more weight and to tire more quickly.

Hypersensitivity unaddressed, can become self-devastating and other-alienating.

Government might do well, both to lighten the financial burden of the excessively wealthy, and to lighten the poverty burden of the excessively poor.

To husband one's resources, is to keep one's nose above the water.

Listen carefully when spoken to, pause briefly, and then answer thoughtfully.

Too many heed, when they should have heeded.

Silent observation is withdrawal, not participation.

Things never are what one would have them be.

Life monetized, is life dehumanized.

Music, dance and song, never fail to attract a happy throng.

Wisdom is a rare consequence of life fully lived both mentally and physically.

To devote oneself exclusively to thought, will quickly leave one very distraught.

Food for thought is plentiful, but thinkers are short in supply.

Change but for change, is playful novelty, change for progress, is a serious cultural matter.

Nature and culture go their separate conflicting ways.

Civility *once* graced the halls of diplomacy.

To be wealthy is good, but to be healthy is better.

To be exceptional is not necessarily to be better.

Money and politics have become close playmates.

Some embrace the gospel of time and multiplicity,
Others the gospel of timelessness and oneness.

In the living, there's a past, present and future.
For the dead, there's no recall and nothing new.

Exercise will your mind and body energize.

To be athletic is to be energetic.

Rest is best, when work is done.

Timidity is asininity, not sublimity.

To be loud, is to be heard more than heeded.

Recreation is good for regeneration.

The nimble are alert and able.

To procrastinate is to chronically hesitate.

Just to counter and not add, is a common exercise in futility.

To the living, life is the all.

Epigrams attract and hold both young and old.

Ill-will is reflexive, good-will is thoughtful.

To some, knowing is good and not-knowing is bad,
To others, the opposite is the case.

Easy paths end in sloth. The choice is yours.

To test oneself as broadly as possible, is to learn to know oneself.

Nature and culture have always gone their separate ways.

Though all has, and will always change, nothing that is, will ever
cease to be.

Mankind's evolution will continue its upward spiral,
Eventually to end in who knows what!
Whence, whither and why, will continue to defy
All human curiosity and intelligence.

Smiles of approval and words of praise,
Self-esteem will foster and raise.

Threats invite opposition, not cooperation.

To identify oneself with a group, is to lose one's identity.

Expect more of yourself than does society at large.

What's in it for me, is a compelling determinant.

A relationship starts to unravel, when it begins to demand more than it gives.

The weak cannot be but humble and meek.

All living things are both hunters and prey.

Too many adults remain children in too many ways.

The female is the indispensable mother of mankind, the male is but a necessary means.

To do is to be, to know is to grow.

Too many humans are inadequately informed, and virtually thoughtless.

Do yourself, think yourself, to become yourself or to be yourself.

Too few humans shape and make themselves, too many allow themselves to be shaped and made by circumstances.

Education enhances life, training supplements income.

Physical muscle is important, mental muscle is imperative.

A new thought a day, boredom will allay.

The world of psychology, paradoxically tends both to the emotional health of the nation and to the financial health of the business world.

Too few grow, most just expand.

To be rich in things alone, is to be poor.

To be wealthy, is of itself not a badge of honor.

The body needs food to eat, and the mind needs bones to gnaw.

Moderation is life's alpha and omega.

Things of the body are earthly, things of the spirit are heavenly.

Things cannot renew themselves, bodies do.

On earth, humans are rancor and strife, in heaven, they are sweetness and light!

The ordinary and normal attract little attention, the unusual and deviant command attention.

Life in brief: toil, trouble and grief.

Art appears to be whatever is deemed to be art.

Punishment is retribution, not atonement.

People are something between what they think they are, and what others think they are.

Choice and chance are partners in life's dance.

Leave your footprint, even if but in the sand.

If but a job, one is but a means.

Defer only, when deference is deserved.

Genes and circumstances, make and shape. A passion or two will see one through.

Life is not what it could be or should be, and never will be.

To conflate information, knowledge and wisdom, is to diminish all three.

Better to minimize garbage than to manage it.

To criticize is good, to remedy is better.

Don't conceal, reveal and remedy.

The unusual do the unusual.

What can be commodified and monetized, will so be.

When and where money can be made, it will be made.

Sport, once a general playful world of sundry games, has become a vast lucrative business benefiting but the few.

To rest though not tired, is to become tired.

Loafing dulls the wits and lethargizes the body.

To fail repeatedly, is to succeed eventually.

To fail is to learn painfully.

Better to be, than but to seem to be.

Life ruffles, death levels.

The chariot wheels of time roll rough-shod over the face of reality.

The familiar breeds indifference, the different stirs curiosity.

Strife is the name of life.

Hope and perseverance can overcome resistance.

Immigration revulsion is a common compulsion.

The unknown threatens, the different intrigues.

An alarmingly large number of professionals become their profession to an alarming degree.

Life's niceties are paled by life's crudities.

To make popular, one need only ban.

Trials and tribulations, make or break.

Nothing is, but that it is constantly changing, slowly or rapidly, imperceptibly or visibly.

Retribution is sweet revenge, not a solution.

The unconventional of today, becomes the norm of tomorrow.

Today's possibilities become tomorrow's realities.

When reason weakens, insanity beckons.

Too much technology, spells too little humanity.

Life's flow is a forceful advance, life's ebb is a hesitant retreat.

Mortality is not a disease.

Birth is chance, death is fate.

Fringe changes are common, core changes are rare.

In its extremes, the Electronics Age will depersonalize and dehumanize mankind.

Futility is judgment, not fact.

Epigrams are the philosopher's tweets.

People don't meet, they just tweet.

To dine is fine, to dine and wine is finer.

Happiness is a chance consequence, not a deliberate pursuit.

Too much brain and too little brawn, is no less desirable than too little brain and too much brawn.

Subjectivity is reflexive, objectivity is reflective.

The female is selective, the male compulsive.

Girls look up to their dads, boys are attached to their mothers.

Sexually, women sally and men rush.

Parents and the home are life's major determinants.

Punishment is more retribution than redemption.

Hypersensitivity is a pain that knows no gain.

Life is a challenge, not a problem.

Little is what we humans would have it be.

Wars will not become a memory, until bridges of understanding and appreciation grace the entire surface of our Mother Earth.

Reason contracts, imagination expands.

To teach is to transmit and to explain,

To learn is to absorb and to understand.

Sexual attraction is seductive, sexual interaction is productive.

Begin right, and keep your goal in sight.

Each is fixed in identity, and fluid in being.

What has happened, cannot be unhappened.

Technology has become a religion without a church.

Happiness surfaces with one's unqualified acceptance of self and life.

Ending the old is distressing, starting the new is challenging.

Mankind must change for the better, if the world is ever to become better.

About the Author

Joseph Mileck was born in Sanktmartin, Roumania in 1922, immigrated to Canada in 1926 and again in 1931. He has a B.A. Degree from McMaster University, Hamilton, Ontario (1945), and a PhD. from Harvard University (1950). Joseph was a member of the German Department of the University of California, Berkeley from 1950 to 1991. He has published five books and numerous articles, dealing with such German authors as Franz Kafka, Thomas Mann and Hermann Hesse. He has also edited two cultural-historical books about Sanktmartin, a typical German community in Roumania, and has published a book-length study of that community's dialect. To these scholarly works, published from 1951 to 2003, Joseph has added four collections of his own poetry and epigrams: *A Trail of Poetic Reflection.* Berkeley, California: Beatitude Press, 2008, 114 pp.; *A Medley of Piquant Poetry and Edgy Epigrams.* Berkeley, California: Beatitude Press, 2010, 126 pp.; *More Salt and Pepper. Poems and Epigrams.* Berkeley, California: Beatitude Press, 2012, 173 pp.; and *Pensive Pauses. Epigrams and Poems.* Berkeley, California: Pensive Oasis Press, 2016, 226 pp.

To his many literary bibliographical, linguistic, and socio-political books, Mileck added a critical appraisal of the United States (*America. An Empire in Disarray.* Berkeley, California: Beatitude Press, 2013, 172 pp.), and a collection of topical essays and brief asides (*Essayistic Ventures and Topical Asides.* Berkeley, California: Pensive Oasis press, 2017, 246 pp.).

www.ingramcontent.com/pod-product-compliance
Lightning Source LLC
LaVergne TN
LVHW051510080426
835509LV00017B/2011